Thank you For helping US

LET THEM LIVE

How a Simple Act of Kindness Sparked a Movement

NATHAN BERNING   EMILY BERNING

JOHN GRECO

CONTENTS

Mom, you have ALWAYS been my biggest supporter!

Without your unconditional love and undying support, none of the works described in this book would have been possible.

Thank you for always encouraging me to pursue big dreams with a belief that they can (and will) happen!

FOREWORD

In the world of pro-life authors there are many; however, I am only familiar with one newly married couple who, when they encountered a mom considering an abortion, emptied their bank account to help her. Talk about putting your money where your mouth is.

Nathan and Emily Berning are true start-up founders who have built a movement of generosity, creating a current that is sweeping thousands of people into it. They are serving moms and saving babies from coast to coast. This book tells some of the amazing stories of how it all came to be. They are full of sacrifice, inspiring moms, and a profound approach to supporting life.

In 2011 my wife and I founded Save the Storks, an organization that built sonogram-equipped mobile units to help mothers at the door of an abortion clinic. Some of the moms just need someone to talk to, listen to them and support them... to really listen, without judgment or advice. We had a chance to see, firsthand, moms bond with their baby and as a result, many women chose life.

This experience was beyond anything we had encountered. I was instantly addicted. There is nothing more rewarding than seeing a mom change her mind and love her baby.

And so I understand Nathan and Emily's passion for what they do. When I first met them they had no children, yet their phones were filled with photos of beautiful babies and mothers that they had saved.

At our last meeting at the March For Life, they were proudly carrying around the most beautiful baby girl in the pinkest outfit I've ever seen. Nathan and Emily said, "This is Ayla, and we might get to adopt her." Their charity invested in Ayla's mom, helping her with her rent and providing the cushion she needed to choose life and carry Ayla to term. To meet Ayla and hear her story, you could not help but tear up. There is no doubt that Ayla was worth it.

In an extraordinary way this book is not just about life but also about wealth. As I read it, I kept asking the question, "How much is one life worth?" To the Berning family, one life is worth everything... because they understand that there is another kind of wealth, one that cannot be lost or taken away.

Remember the story of the woman who found the treasure in the field? Once she discovered it she went and compelled everyone to join her in buying up that field. That is what Let Them Live and their One Life movement is all about. Nathan and Emily have found that field, and they are inviting you to join them. May their story, conviction, and courage inspire you —as it has me—to join with them in giving all for that treasure!

Joe Baker
Founder, Save the Storks

INTRODUCTION

Imagine, if you can, getting a phone call from your oldest son, who's newly married, self-employed and living in a recreational vehicle. "I did something big last night mom!" The big thing he did was to take all the money in his checking account and wire it to someone living in another country. "I met this woman online who was frantically trying to help her cousin not have an abortion. I felt called to help her mom, so we sent her all of our money!"

In my head, I was screaming "how about helping yourself...from starving or freezing to death this winter in your RV!!" I don't remember exactly what I said, but it wasn't anything encouraging that he wanted to hear like, that's great son! I'm so proud of you! Etc, etc. No, I just couldn't believe he had sent all his money (and his new wife's as well) without even checking to make sure that this woman was even real... that she really had a pregnant cousin who was threatening to have an abortion. What in the world was he thinking?!!

Now, Nathan has always been one to make speedy and sometimes rash decisions in the past, but this one seemed, even to me, his biggest fan and supporter, to be reckless and maybe even dangerous.

Fast forward four years and over 600 babies saved from abortion later, and I'm finding it incredibly hard to find the right words to say. I am proud, for sure, but it's more than that, way more than that. What Nathan and Emily have done and are doing is changing the world. They're helping frightened mothers who desperately want to have their babies, have them! They're meeting these moms where they are on their journeys and helping to alleviate their burdens. Some of the moms just need someone to talk to, listen to them and support them...to really listen, without judgment or advice.

Have there been a few bumps in the road along the way? For sure. But those bumps have helped them to learn and grow Let Them Live into the organization that it is today. Now, I'm so glad that Nathan listened to his heart and made that initially reckless decision and that Emily, without hesitation, said YES to it!

Rebecca Berning
Nathan's Mom

CHAPTER 1

TO SAVE A LIFE

"Do you want to save a life?" It was a simple question, but it was one that changed everything for us—and, as it turned out, for countless others too.

It was three in the morning on Saturday, December 1. Emily and I were staying in the guest room of my grandfather's home in Michigan as part of an extended holiday with the family. In the darkness of that room, I lay awake in bed, unable to fall asleep. I'm one of those people who doesn't rest easily; it seems the more I do, the more energy I have. So it wasn't unusual for me to be awake, scrolling through social media on my phone, with Emily fast asleep next to me.

Scanning through comments on a pro-life page, I read a message that made me want to cry. It said:

distant cousin good friends but sadly she muchly needs to get her life straightened out I went down family path she went down drugs booze and sex path leading to 3 abortions one being scheduled for next week

Next week? I knew I needed to do something to try and get this mother to change her mind. I reached out to the woman who posted the message—Abbie was her name—and we began texting back and forth. She told me that her cousin was at a low point in her life. She had lost custody of her other two children, and they had become wards of the state. She also lost her job and had been evicted from her apartment. As a result, she was now living in a van, braving temperatures that could reach single digits at night. Having another child seemed out of the question.

My instincts told me to adopt the baby. Emily and I had no children of our own, and we would gladly take in this precious life. Maybe if the mother knew someone else was willing to raise the child, she'd be willing to carry her baby to term. I told Abbie we'd like to adopt the baby and that if the mother canceled her appointment for an abortion, we'd send her a thousand dollars right away. I knew it wasn't much, but it was most of our savings.

I explained that my wife and I had started a pro-life organization called Let Them Live. We were serious about trying to save every baby we could.

Abbie texted her cousin, whose name was Debbie, I discovered. I waited anxiously for the reply. When it came, my stomach churned. Debbie said, "I don't adopt. It's either keep or throw away." *Throw away?* I was fine with her not wanting us to adopt. More than anything, though, I wanted her to cancel her appointment and let her baby live.

I texted back: "I can give her $1,000 if she'll cancel that appointment. I can send to her through PayPal or Venmo." Again, I waited for her to share the message with her cousin.

Two minutes later, three little dots appeared on my phone screen to tell me a response was coming. "I will keep this ball of cells for $1,250. I doubt it's legit though."

Twelve hundred and fifty dollars was everything we had in our bank account, but I was willing to give it to a woman I'd never met before if it meant we could save her unborn baby from an abortion. I knew Emily would feel the same way, so I turned and gently nudged her from her sleep. After all, I was about to give away all our money.

Only half-roused, she looked up at me with curiosity in her eyes. "Do you want to save a life?" I asked her. I held up my phone. "It will cost us twelve hundred and fifty dollars, but this woman won't go through with the abortion she has scheduled for Monday morning if we give her the money."

Emily didn't need to think about it. "Of course," she said. "Whatever we need to do to save the baby."

I kissed Emily on the forehead and turned my eyes back to my phone to respond. I told my new pro-life ally I'd gladly pay her cousin twelve hundred and fifty dollars if she would look up pictures of a twelve-week-old fetus and cancel her appointment.

After that, there was a bit of back-and-forth. Debbie wanted to make sure we weren't trying to scam her somehow. I explained that everything I'd said was completely sincere. Once again, I told her that my wife and I were part of the pro-life movement, and we were serious about doing whatever it took to save the life of her unborn baby.

After several minutes of conversation through our mediator, I finally received the text I'd been hoping for:

She says, Do you know if I can cancel on a Saturday or would I have to go in to cancel Monday?

I breathed an audible sigh of relief. Emily and I were over-the-moon thrilled, completely ecstatic to know this baby had been saved. But the most exciting moment came a few days later when I received another text. It was an ultrasound picture of Debbie's seven-week-old unborn baby—a baby with a future.

~

It was so simple. We were able to save a life without changing a single law or picketing a single abortion facility. All we had to do was ask what the child's mother needed in order to choose life instead of an abortion, and then meet that need. In this case, it turned out to be twelve hundred and fifty dollars. Compared to the value of a human life, that's nothing.

Of course, there's nothing wrong with using the levers of politics or protest to effect change. When we first began Let Them Live, we were focused on state and federal laws and policies. We were involved in raising support for Michigan's heartbeat bill and had traveled to Washington, D.C. for the March for Life. We'd even traveled to Ireland for the fight to save the Eighth Amendment, which protected the lives of the unborn. I thought politics would be the way we would make the greatest difference in the pro-life movement. Today, after the overturning of *Roe v. Wade*, these approaches are still incredibly important—some might even argue they've become more important—but because of my late-night texting adventure a few years ago, I now understand there is another way.

Several weeks after my encounter with Abbie and her cousin, Emily and I went to see the film *Schindler's List*. It had been brought back to theaters for its twenty-fifth anniversary, and I had never seen it before. Only a handful of movies have made me cry. This was one of them.

The true story takes place in German-occupied Poland and Czechoslovakia during World War II; and revolves around

Oskar Schindler, a coldhearted German businessman who appears to care more about money than people. But then something shifts. As the reality of the Holocaust takes hold and Schindler witnesses Jews being gunned down in the streets, he begins using his wealth and influence to save as many lives as possible. His strategy is simple: employ Jews—lots of them—so he can save them from the concentration camps. Saving lives becomes his obsession. He spends everything he has rescuing all that he can over the course of the war.

In the end, Oskar Schindler saves more than eleven hundred Jews. Though he is grief-stricken that he couldn't save more, the Jewish workers in his factory recognize what he has done for them. They present him with a ring engraved with a quotation from the Jewish Talmud: "Whoever saves one life saves the world entire."

As Emily and I watched the final scenes of the film with tears in our eyes, we both realized Oskar Schindler was onto something—something that would reshape Let Them Live forever. Schindler didn't try to change the Nazis' minds about the Jewish people. He didn't try to effect change with protests in the streets. But he didn't put his head down and ignore the plight of those who were suffering either. Schindler figured out a straightforward and simple way to save lives. He used his money to employ Jewish men and women, thereby saving them from the concentration camps. He paid what it took to save a life, and then he did it again and again and again.

I knew this was the approach we needed to take at Let Them Live. It had worked with Abbie's cousin, and I believed it could work with other mothers. According to the Guttmacher Institute, 73% of abortions happen for financial reasons.[1] In other words, nearly three quarters of women who seek an abortion do so because they do not believe they have the resources necessary to provide for their unborn child. That means more than seven out of every ten abortions in the United States can be prevented if those financial needs can be met. Imagine if every pro-life person in America decided to chip in and help. Imagine how many lives could be saved. Imagine how many moms could avoid the anguish of post-abortion depression and lifelong regret. Imagine how many stories of sadness could be transformed into stories of joy.

Behind every abortion statistic are real mothers—real women in desperate situations, many of whom don't know where to turn for help. Emily and I decided that Let Them Live would focus on those women—all those who believe that, because of their financial limitations, they have no choice but to schedule an abortion and end their pregnancy.

In the grand scheme of things, money is worth so very little when placed next to a human life. As it was with Oskar Schindler, saving lives has become something of an obsession —and it's one that seems to take hold of every donor, partner, counselor, and advocate who joins us in this work.

I recognize that it can sound very cold to weigh the life of an unborn child against a monetary donation. That first baby Emily and I saved with the money in our bank account— twelve hundred and fifty dollars—was just the beginning. But as we would learn in the months that followed, it takes more than money to change the world one person at a time.

In the spring of 2019, Let Them Live was formally converted into a non-profit organization. Rather than focusing on changing laws or winning elections, we set out to revive Oskar Schindler's strategy of saving lives. In the months that followed, we did just that. Through crowdfunding, we saved several more babies from being aborted. Typically, we offered the mothers a few hundred dollars in gift cards for food and baby supplies, plus rent for a month or two. That was all it took for these women to choose life instead of a Planned Parenthood appointment. I was struck by how little it took to pull someone out of their hopelessness. A few thousand dollars' worth of help, and these women were ready to avoid one of the biggest and most tragic decisions anyone can make.

Emily and I thought we knew the road that lay ahead of us, but we never could have imagined where it would lead. In the beginning, we depended on the kindness of friends and family. Before long, though, we were connecting willing donors with women teetering toward abortion to pull them back from the brink. It was all so simple but so powerful. And then we met a woman who changed all that. Her name was Margaret, and she showed us that life is more complicated than we first imagined. Together, we learned that money is a great start, but it can't be the end.

At the 2019 San Francisco Pro-Life Conference we met J. C., a sidewalk counselor from 40 Days for Life, a Christian ministry that works on the front lines of the pro-life move-ment, offering prayer and counseling to women entering Planned Parenthood and other abortion facilities. She told us about Margaret, whom she had met several days before. Margaret hadn't yet gone through with her abortion, but her situation was desperate.

Margaret had been a prostitute and an exotic dancer. She was estranged from her family, and the father of her unborn child had left her. Though she had left the sex industry months earlier, she had recently been let go of her nine-to-five job. Now, she was nineteen weeks pregnant and living in her car. While her heart told her she would regret the decision for the rest of her life, she felt abortion was her only option.

We reached out to Margaret and offered her a three-hundred-dollar Wal-Mart gift card, a hotel room while she looked for a place to live, and two months of rent once she did. Margaret agreed not to have the abortion. She told us she had been hoping God would show up and save her from having to go through with it. It seemed we were the answer to her prayers. Emily and I were thrilled.

But then something changed. As the weeks passed by, Margaret faced the realization that she needed more than a one- or two-month housing solution. She also needed more than a few hundred dollars to spend on diapers and baby clothes at a big box store. Her baby—a son, she had learned—would be her responsibility until he was an adult. The weight of all she would need to provide hit her with the force of a freight train. And so, she decided she needed to have the abortion after all. But first, she texted me:

Hey. Just reaching out before I go through with my appointment on Thurs/Fri. I felt like I had some real support. . . But I've really sunk into a bad place mentally.

I don't want to live with the pain and guilt of my choices. . . I don't want to live at all. I thought God would be there so much more than this.

Thank you for trying to help me. I'll send you back the gift card when it arrives. I'm so sorry.

I read these words slowly, making sure she was actually saying what I thought she was saying. I showed them to Emily. We were both heartbroken. We wanted to reach out and hug Margaret, this woman who had, over a very short period, become a friend to us. Mostly, we wanted her to know

God hadn't abandoned her—and neither would we. I texted back:

Hey Margaret! It isn't true that you don't have support!! God does love you, and this is his answer to your prayers.

We want to help you. It's not our money. It belongs to you, and your baby.

I then called Margaret and told her, at the very least, we wanted the chance to help her. Then I told her that Emily and I were packing our bags. We were going to come see her, and we'd be there tomorrow. Emily and I didn't go to bed that night. Instead, we drove two hours from our home in Fort Wayne to the Indianapolis International Airport so that we could catch the next available flight to Sacramento.

When we met up with Margaret, she gave each of us a big hug, and there were tears in her eyes. She told us she just couldn't believe we'd drop everything and fly all the way to California for her. It was clear to me she wasn't used to this kind of friendship, this kind of unconditional support. Of this moment, Margaret would later say, "Truly understanding that I'm not alone, that I have support, and that God really was there—and He is there... it was my turning point." And it was.

Margaret decided that she was going to continue with her pregnancy. Despite life's challenges, she was going to have her baby. Abortion was no longer going to be an option for her. And we were very grateful to help her in whatever way we could.

The truth is, we didn't have a plan. We didn't know how much support Margaret would need to get back on her feet; we just knew she wasn't there yet, and an unborn life hung in the balance. Margaret was unlike most of the mothers we had helped up to that point and since. While most of the moms we meet want to choose life but don't know how to make ends meet, Margaret's decision wasn't as certain. And so, while she wavered from time to time, we made our commitment simple: we would be there to come alongside her and provide whatever assistance she needed, before the birth and afterwards.

On March 2, 2020, Margaret gave birth to a beautiful baby boy, whom she named Stephen. Emily and I were blessed to be in the delivery room to welcome him into this world. It's hard to describe the joy I felt holding that precious baby in my arms. I know Emily felt the same joy. And as promised, Let Them Live's support didn't stop once Stephen came. We continued to raise funding to assist Margaret as she adjusted to life as a single mom.

With all that Margaret had to worry about in those days, there was one struggle she hadn't counted on—a global pandemic. Just as she was introducing Stephen to the world, the world was beginning to shut down. Stores and restaurants closed. Businesses stopped hiring. People were locked down in their homes. In California, especially, it was hard for someone on the margins like Margaret to survive. So, Margaret decided her family of two needed a change of scenery. In June of 2020, Margaret and Stephen boarded a plane bound for Indiana. They stayed with us in our home, and I found Margaret work for the summer.

Berning Trailer Sales has been our family business for generations. My grandfather sold new Airstream and Shasta travel trailers. When I was a teenager, I realized I could make a bit of money by refurbishing used trailers. In fact, years later it was the money I earned flipping Airstream travel trailers that allowed Emily and me to buy our home—but that's a story for another chapter. I had recently purchased a very used Airstream that needed quite a bit of refurbishing. But since I knew Margaret could use whatever money I'd be able to earn in the process, I gave her the travel trailer. She worked all summer, replacing the vinyl flooring, repairing the trim work, painting the interior, and replacing the cabinet fronts. I think she was grateful to have a mission, something she could accomplish for her son. In the end, she made nine thousand dollars for her efforts.

As the summer wound down, Margaret had a new spirit about her. Though we would have been happy to have her and Stephen stay with us for good—they had both become like part of our family—Margaret told us she was ready to return to California with her son and try again. She'd patched up her relationship with her father, and he had invited her and Stephen to come and stay with him. Margaret was eager to take a step forward. She wanted to go back to school to complete a degree in interior design, and it seemed like the right time.

We had grown rather attached to the thought of Margaret and Stephen being a part of our lives. Stephen had just started crawling, and it hurt to think we wouldn't be around when he reached his next milestone. It was difficult to say goodbye, so perhaps it was a good thing that when the time came, Emily and I were out of town. We bought Margaret and Stephen plane tickets, lent her a car to drive to the airport, and said goodbye from a distance. Margaret had earned nine thousand dollars that summer, and because of the federal government's COVID stimulus check program, she had more money waiting for her back home. She was ready to start again.

In truth, so were we. Margaret and Stephen helped Emily and me to realize Let Them Live needed to do more than provide a shot of financial help to women in crisis. We needed to help them create a sustainable path into the future. This path might include a new budget, job training, a career change, or a different housing situation. All that takes time, and that means the financial support, the counseling, and the coaching we offer would have to be increased and prolonged in many cases. It also meant we would need to invest more in understanding each and every situation. Every case is unique because every mom is unique. We've made it a goal never to forget that.

When we meet a pregnant woman in need, our goal is to bring whatever help she needs so that she can choose life and do so confidently. More times than not, a difficult life has convinced these women that no one is going to take care of them, that no one is going to help when things go south. We've seen this same fear in the eyes of hundreds of women. Sadly, this is one thing most of these moms have in common. Let Them Live exists to let these women know this fear welling up inside of them is lying to them. There *are* people who care. There *are* people who are willing to provide whatever resources are needed. There *are* people who want to help them get back on their feet so they can lead a good and meaningful life with the child God has given to them.

As I write this, Let Them Live has saved nearly six hundred babies from abortion. Each one is precious. Each one is special. Each one is made in the image of God. This work is so very important—perhaps the most important work there is. I say this not to pat myself on the back but because what they told Oskar Schindler really is true: "Whoever saves one life saves the world entire."

CHAPTER 2

HOW TO BE PRO-LIFE

Good Samaritans don't get to pick and choose whom they help: they meet the needs of anyone who crosses their path. It doesn't matter if that person is black or white, rich or poor, has a criminal record or perfect Sunday school attendance. The need is all that matters.

On some level we all know this, and yet we live in a world that divides people into tribes. We use superficial traits like religion, race, geography, and socio-economic status to classify people as "one of us" or "one of them." Most of us don't even know we're doing it. There seems to be something in the deepest parts of a person's soul, the place where insecurities and anxieties reside, prompting them to look for similarities and connections. We tend to reach out to people we can easily relate to, and sadly, we are tempted to cross to the other side of the street when the person in need is someone from another tribe.

I can't say I was born without the same tendencies and preferences as other people. But some of the life choices my parents made as I was growing up turned out to be a tremendous gift to me. They allowed me to feel out of place, to be the one on the outside, to experience an unfamiliar culture and see the beauty in it. I tell you this not because I consider myself inoculated from prejudice, as though I were somehow unique. Rather, I bring it up because to be truly pro-life a person must set aside the very idea of tribalism.

There is no religious requirement to work with Let Them Live. Mothers don't need to affirm a statement of faith or anything like that. We welcome anyone in need. We also don't ask our employees to agree with us on spiritual matters either. We're willing to work with anyone who believes in our mission. In fact, we have several donors who identify as pro-choice. They recognize that our work gives women the freedom to choose, and they're happy to see them choose life if that's what they really want.

Moms considering an abortion come from all backgrounds and walks of life. Good Samaritans don't get to interview the stranger on the side of the road and ask about their life choices before deciding whether to help. They don't assess a person based on the way they look. They don't consider whether the person in need is a member of their tribe. All they see is the humanity of the person lying there. All they are concerned about is the need and how they can meet it.

When I was eight years old, my family moved out to the west coast. My dad—at the time, a physician in training—was offered a fellowship at the Buncke Clinic in San Francisco. For a year he learned about microvascular surgery techniques, and the rest of us learned about life in a different part of the country.

For me, the adjustment wasn't just regional. Mine was a cross-cultural experience. While we were living in San Francisco, my brother and I attended a public school where nearly all the students were Chinese. Other than a few whites and Hispanics, everyone in the school—the students, the teachers, the administrators—were all Chinese. I had never been a minority before, but suddenly I was. I didn't know it at the time, but I was the first white student my teacher, Miss Hong, had ever had in her classroom.

Overall, my experience wasn't a bad one. The education I received that year was better than anything I'd received up to that point and better than what I would later receive when my family relocated to my parents' hometown of Fort Wayne, Indiana. But it wasn't just that the standards were unusually high: it was that the teachers really cared about their students. From what I could see, they took a personal interest in each one, trying to unlock their unique potential so they could succeed. Rather than simply making sure the class as a whole was keeping up with the assignments and the lessons, these teachers challenged and helped each student to keep growing academically, regardless of where the state or the assigned curriculum said they "should" be. And of course, that included me.

That kind of pressure takes some getting used to, and I didn't always handle it well. I recall one day on the playground losing it on another kid. To be fair, this other kid was a bit of a bully. I wanted to play basketball, and he wouldn't let me have the ball. He and the other kids with him were teasing me—and all in Mandarin. I was the odd man out, the one who didn't quite fit in, and they made sure I knew it. I remember they were all laughing at me. I grabbed the ball, and the bully pulled it right back. So, I did what I thought I needed to do at the time. I let every ounce of rage out, and I began kicking him in the shin as hard as I could.

A teacher quickly pulled me away and brought me inside

the school. I knew I was in trouble. What I remember most vividly was how seriously everyone took the incident. It wasn't just a playground fight between two boys. There was no "boys will be boys" excuse offered. In fact, there were no excuses of any kind offered. Miss Hong calmly and gravely explained to me that such behavior was not only wrong but illegal. It would not be tolerated at John Yehall Chin Elementary school. It could not happen again. My third-grade self took it all in, and I hung my head. Tears rolled down my cheeks, and all I could think was, *I don't want to go to jail!*

Of course, I didn't go to jail that day, but I did feel the weight of my poor choices. Just as I had been challenged academically in this environment, I was now being challenged to develop the sort of character I could be proud of. It was another part of the cultural shift I was experiencing. It's not that the teachers at other schools didn't care about their students' character; it was just taken to another level at a school brimming with Chinese culture. Discipline and personal development were deeply ingrained, and it came through loud and clear.

That year in a sea of Chinese faces passed by quickly, but it left an indelible mark on my life. Looking back, it was something of a gift. I learned there is beauty to be found in other cultures, and there's no reason to be afraid of people who looked or sounded different than me. I learned what it feels like to be on the outside. I learned that race is only skin deep. I learned that this world is a lot bigger than what I had experienced up to that point. And I learned that caring for other people is not a one-size-fits-all sort of thing. Every person has a story to be learned; every person has the potential to do great things.

∼

A few years later, I found myself surrounded by an even larger sea of Chinese faces. When I was thirteen, my parents brought my brother and me to Guangzhou, China. We were there to adopt a baby girl named Chen Kangqi, my then soon-to-be sister, Lily. Finalizing the adoption process was no small task, so we stayed in-country for weeks.

It's difficult to say what surprised me the most about China. I suppose it was simply how different it was from the United States. I remember the traffic—how cars traveled down main streets without true travel lanes, swerving in and out and around one another, every transition a near-miss. I remember people walking and biking and pushing carts across vast, unmarked intersections, indifferent to the cars and buses shooting by them. I remember the sights and smells of the wet markets, livestock everywhere, fish hanging from the rafters. I remember people eating strange critters like water beetles and eating curdled horse blood. I remember buying a case of beer from the corner market and drinking from it legally, because there was no drinking age.

I also remember the way the people we met talked about life. We hear a lot about the Chinese Communist Party's single-child policy and the forced abortions imposed on the people of China; but those who uphold the old traditions cherish life, so much so that in mainland China, the people actually account for a person's age by including the nine months they spent in the womb. No one doubts that life really does begin at conception. When you're a kid, every year counts, so while we were in China I loved being able to say I was fourteen rather than thirteen.

Mostly, though, I remember the way the people related to one another, the way they treated us. For one, we stood out. Being white, somewhat tall, and wearing Western clothes, we didn't exactly fade into the background. But that was okay.

The Chinese were very welcoming. Most people seemed glad to see us. There was one woman who saw our little group—our family and a few others, all in China to adopt—and decided we must be the answer to her prayers. We were walking down a busy street when she came running up to us. She kneeled in front of my dad and one of the other Americans we were there with, and she held up her baby. She wanted us to take her infant daughter with us back to the United States; she wanted us to give her a better life. It was heartbreaking.

I tugged on my dad's sleeve and told him, "We should take the baby." It seemed to me the right thing to do. We could help this poor child; we could give this woman the peace she wanted. Of course, Dad couldn't just take this stranger's baby and bring her back to America. There were rules and laws to prevent that very thing. To this day, there is an image stuck in my mind of this poor woman, so desperate to provide for her daughter that she was willing to give her up. She didn't ask us for money. She wasn't looking for a handout. Her only concern was her child. It's hard to imagine the sort of pain she must have been experiencing.

A short time later, we arrived at the adoption center in Changsha to meet Lily for the first time. She was just eleven months old—not yet old enough to know what was about to happen but certainly old enough to know that she was being held by people she didn't know. Even so, she didn't fuss or cry. She just rested in my dad's arms, perfectly content. Right from the start, Lily just fit into our family. We knew it, and apparently so did she.

～

Growing up with my little sister, Lily, there was no place to draw boundaries based on race or geography. There was never a point when I considered Lily somehow less than my sister. There's no asterisk next to her in my heart. Adoption is a magical thing. Somehow, in the love that flows through a family, a child is grafted in, as though they were there all along, always meant to be a part, forever bound as an heir of that family's legacy. They say blood is thicker than water, but there is something thicker even than blood; it's the love that brings people into the same story. It happens in marriage, of course, but it can happen through the bond of adoption as well.

I began this chapter by saying that everyone who considers themselves pro-life must be a Good Samaritan. They cannot pass by on the other side of the street when they see a need. It simply won't do to care for the life of an unborn child if they don't also care for the life of the mother in dire straits. For Emily and me, this desire to love the lost and help the hurting extends to the point that we have decided that if the only way to save a child and put the mother's mind at ease is to adopt, so be it. Our lives and our house are open to children who need a home.

At Let Them Live, we know that no two situations are the same, but in no situation is an abortion the right answer. Our goal is to help mothers get past the feeling of being overwhelmed, to push through the fog of hopelessness to discover that the child growing in their womb is a blessing and not a curse. And so, what we do is quite simple. Let Them Live eases some of the financial burden by crowdfunding donations. Then, one of our counselors will help an expectant mother develop a life plan for the next few years so there's a path forward once the child is born. Often, it's here that we see the look of despair disappear from a mother's face. In its place is a look of excitement as they await their new baby. But sometimes, no matter what we are able to offer, a woman will still tell us they're not ready to be a mom.

In these cases, adoption may be the answer. Adoption is a way for a mom to choose life and secure a loving home for her child when she doesn't feel equipped to care for a baby herself. Adoption has been a beautiful part of my own story, so I know it can be a beautiful option for these moms, most of whom hate the idea of abortion, even if it seems like their only choice.

When Emily and I met Mary a few years back, she was pregnant with twins. She had planned to have an abortion, because she and her husband didn't know how they could provide for a baby—let alone two—in the midst of their financial challenges. Mary was referred to Let Them Live, and she found a bit of hope. Immediate financial relief helped relieve their burden, and knowing there were people who cared enough to help her and her husband get back on their feet gave Mary the courage to choose life for her babies. She came to us uncertain and afraid, and within a few short weeks, she was a beaming mom-to-be, looking forward to welcoming her twins into this world.

Tragically, Mary never got to bring her babies home from the hospital. She suffered a miscarriage at 10 weeks. In the days that followed, we mourned with Mary. We knew how far she had come. We knew how her heart had made room for those twins, and now, of course, there was a vacancy left by their absence. Even though her story didn't end like we had all hoped, I was proud of Mary. She had chosen life. She had chosen to stand and fight for her babies—and no loss could take that away from her.

Here's the thing, though. Mary didn't just choose life for her unborn twins. She chose life for herself. She chose to step up and make a plan. She chose to take hold of her future. And she chose to be a light to help others find their way. A short while after she recovered from her miscarriage, Mary came back to Let Them Live. This time, however, it wasn't for help with a pregnancy: she decided she wanted to give back, to serve women just like her who feel afraid and overwhelmed. Today, Mary is one of our most passionate pregnancy counselors. She connects with mothers-to-be and shows them how they, too, can choose life. The women who come to Let Them Live love Mary. Her smile and her concern are genuine. She loves the moms she serves, and she is making a real difference in their lives. So far, not a single mom Mary has counseled has gone through with a planned abortion. She welcomes each baby in honor of the twins she never got to hold.

Not very long ago, Mary counseled a woman named Jamie. When Jamie was referred to Let Them Live, she was 24 weeks pregnant and was convinced she didn't want to be a mother. She didn't think she could handle all that would be required of her to care for her baby. Even so, Jamie allowed us to show her how it could be possible. We conducted a fundraiser for Jamie and took care of many of her bills. Mary worked with Jamie to create action steps to prepare for life once the baby came. Jamie was reluctant, but she was on board. She chose life and gave birth to a beautiful baby girl named Lucy.

Of course, that's not the end of Jamie's story. We rejoice when a baby is born to one of our moms, but we know it's just the beginning. At Let Them Live, we work hard to make sure new mothers have everything they need to succeed. We follow up regularly and let them know they have our support should they need it. It was during one of these follow-ups that Mary discovered Jamie had placed Lucy in daycare. That's fairly normal, especially with working moms. But Jamie had placed Lucy in a non-profit daycare program that also offered overnight respite—and she was leaving her baby daughter there often.

Because Jamie was allowing other people to watch her little girl so frequently and for so long, this other non-profit organization began talking to Jamie about the possibility of letting someone adopt Lucy. Jamie was conflicted; she knew she needed help—and a lot of it—but she didn't want to give Lucy up entirely. She didn't want to miss out on her daughter's life. It was a big decision, and Molly was there to lend an ear and help Jamie see all her options.

Tasha, another one of our counselors at Let Them Live, was available to do quite a bit of babysitting, and Mary arranged for Lucy to spend time with her. This gave Jamie the freedom to really think about her future without the pressure from the other non-profit to give her daughter up for adoption. After some time and without the pressure, however, Jamie began to like the idea of adoption. Even though she knew she had done the right thing by choosing life, she still didn't want to raise Lucy. She wanted the freedom to work and to travel. At the same time, she didn't want to lose Lucy; she still wanted to have a connection with her daughter. Jamie decided an open adoption might be the right choice for her. She would know that Lucy was being cared for, and she would still get to watch her grow up.

A Good Samaritan doesn't get to judge the choices of the people he meets. He simply steps in to offer practical love where love is needed. Emily and I have told Jamie that we would be happy to give Lucy a home. We also told her we would welcome her involvement in Lucy's life if she chose to let us adopt her. There was no pressure from us, of course. We didn't fundraise to provide for Jamie in the hopes of adopting her child. But Emily and I are more than excited about the prospect of giving Lucy the life she deserves. At the time of this writing, Lucy is about twelve weeks old, and we are awaiting Jamie's decision about the adoption. Whatever she ends up deciding, we will support her.

When I think about Jamie, I remember my time in that Chinese school and what it felt like to know I had the support of people who really cared about me; I hope Jamie knows we only want the best for her and baby Lucy. I also think about that poor woman who came up to our group on the streets of Guangzhou and pleaded for us to take her child. I wanted my dad to tell her, "Yes, we will rescue your baby. We will care for your daughter. Don't you worry—we'll make sure she's alright." I now know all the reasons why he couldn't do that. But today, Emily and I have the wonderful privilege of being able to look Jamie in the eye and tell her, "Yes, we will take Lucy. We will care for her as our own. Don't you worry—we'll give her all the love we know you want her to have."

CHAPTER 3

MORE POWERFUL THAN PROPAGANDA

When Emily and I arrived in Ireland with some friends in the spring of 2018, we knew we might face some opposition, but we weren't quite prepared for the backlash we received. We were there to support the pro-life movement in Ireland at a critical moment in history. A landmark vote was going to take place in just a few weeks, and it would quite literally decide the fate of thousands of babies each year.

Ireland has had a long history of protecting the unborn. Elective abortion had been subject to criminal penalties since at least 1861. And in October of 1983, the nation's constitution was amended to outlaw all abortions except in cases where the mother's life is in jeopardy. For thirty-five years, the Eighth Amendment stood as a strong tower, defending those who cannot defend themselves. Sadly, however, for as long as this provision has been in place, there have been people trying to demolish this tower—and in 2018, they made another attempt to repeal the amendment.

The main thrust behind the push to remove the Eighth Amendment from Ireland's constitution came from a single story. Savita Halappanavar was a dentist living in Ireland. In 1992, she died of sepsis after being denied a medically necessary abortion. Pro-abortion advocates will tell you if abortion had been legal in Ireland, Savita would still be alive. What they will fail to tell you, however, is that the doctors treating Savita were not following Irish law when they denied her the procedure. They will also fail to admit that when Savita needed the abortion, it was *after* the baby in her womb had died; she had already experienced a miscarriage.

Under the Eighth Amendment, a medically necessary abortion to save the life of the mother was permitted. What Savita needed—a D&C to clean out her uterus after her miscarriage—was fully permitted. Her case, tragic as it was, was not evidence that Ireland's laws against abortion were dangerous; rather, it was evidence that the doctors treating her were negligent. Even so, public sentiment against the Eighth grew, and by 2018 it seemed pro-choice groups would finally get their dream of an Ireland where abortion on demand is permitted across the land.

At the time, Let Them Live was in its infancy, and our strategy was still political in nature. We focused on policy and legislation, hoping that by changing laws, we could save lives. With ten thousand dollars raised from a GoFundMe campaign, we winged our way to Ireland in time to knock on doors, pass out flyers, and hang posters wherever we could. We stayed for the final month of the campaign. We wanted as many people as possible to know the vote wasn't *really* about women's health, personal freedom, or limited government. It was about the unborn having the same human rights as the rest of us. So we campaigned. We talked to people and advocated for the cause. We wore GoPro cameras everywhere we went to document what we were seeing but also for our own safety and security.

And people threw eggs at us and cussed us out.

It wasn't long before we were featured on the front page of CNN.com. The story essentially painted us as American agitators meddling in Ireland's cultural moment. We didn't care, of course. We assumed negative press would be part of the territory whenever we took a stand. But we were surprised when pro-life groups in Ireland asked us to keep our distance. We had come to help them, and most didn't seem to want our help. Perhaps they worried that our involvement might be seen as foreign interference in Ireland's elections. I could understand their hesitation, so I wasn't mad that we were pushed to the fringes. Mostly, I was disappointed that our impact might be dulled since we were essentially being forced to go it alone.

In the final days before the vote, we canvassed town centers around Dublin with more than five thousand flyers. These flyers featured an image of a twelve-week-old fetus and the simple message "Say NO to abortion on demand!" We wanted people to know that this vote was about more than clumps of cells; it was about babies with arms and legs and beating hearts. Though Ireland did vote to repeal the Eighth Amendment—a devastating loss—we later discovered that in the districts where we campaigned, the "No" votes were five percentage points higher on average. At the very least, we had helped to change some minds.

There were many lessons I took away from our trip to Ireland, but there was one thing I just couldn't get over: the power of propaganda. Savita Halappanavar was not a victim of an unjust law; the lack of abortion on demand on the Emerald Isle wasn't to blame for her untimely death. Reports indicate she died because of simple medical malpractice. Sadly, she's not alone. Many people die because of a doctor's negligence or poor decisions. But because the necessary D&C procedure is sometimes referred to as an abortion, pro-abortion advocates latched on to it and spread the false narrative that Savita died because she couldn't get an abortion when she wanted one. She became the face of the pro-abortion movement. A vote to repeal the Eighth was a vote to save young women just like Savita. But of course, a vote to repeal the Eighth was really a vote to end the lives of more than five thousand innocent babies every year.

A few months after we returned to the States, I heard about a unique bill that had been making the rounds in the Ohio state legislature. Pro-life advocate Janet Porter came up with the idea for the Heartbeat Bill, as it came to be known. It essentially said that if a fetal heartbeat could be detected, then the baby growing in their mother's womb must be afforded the same civil rights and liberties the rest of us enjoy, including full protection from harm. For nearly two decades, Janet had been trying to make the Heartbeat Bill the law of the land in Ohio, but she hadn't been able to make much headway.

I wondered if the bill might find success in another state, so I reached out to a friend of mine in Michigan. Steve Carra worked in the office of Republican State Representative Steve Johnson, and when I told my friend about the Heartbeat Bill, he couldn't wait to tell his boss. Before long, a version of the bill was introduced in the Michigan House and was being debated on the floor. Emily and I knew we had found our next cause to champion, and so we drove up to Michigan in our Suburban with our Airstream in tow. We stayed for more than a month while we tried to drum up support for the fledgling legislation.

It was so simple. Being able to detect a heartbeat showed

the child in the womb was not just some clump of cells. Abortion would stop that beating heart, so of course the baby needed to be protected. I thought about all the lives that would be saved. I thought about how passage of the bill might help people of all stripes see that *abortion* was just another word for murder. But the legislation never made it that far.

To my shock, the fiercest opposition to the bill came from pro-life groups rather than pro-choice organizations. Michigan Right to Life, the little sister organization to the National Right to Life, came out swinging. They denounced the bill as unnecessary and an affront to the true pro-life movement. They argued that Michigan already had some of the strictest anti-abortion laws on the books. The Heartbeat Bill, they said, would only weaken and nullify them. Of course, these laws weren't in effect, because *Roe v. Wade* was still the law of the land. Once *Roe* was overturned, they told us, Michigan would be one of the most pro-life states in the country—without the Heartbeat Bill.

Absent the support of powerful pro-life organizations throughout the state, the Heartbeat Bill failed. Driving home from Michigan, I was once again left with the bitter taste of propaganda in my mouth. Michigan Right to Life branded supporters of the Heartbeat Bill a danger to the pro-life movement. They said we were trying to saddle Michigan with a law that would allow abortion in the early weeks of pregnancy, essentially creating a "pro-abortion loophole" if *Roe* was ever overturned. But the truth was, the Heartbeat Bill was always a stop-gap measure, a way to protect many babies in the womb until such a time when *Roe* could be toppled.

Emily and I were crushed, but it was our twin experiences in Ireland and Michigan that caused us to rethink our approach to the pro-life cause. Pulling on the levers of power can change behavior and, in the case of abortion legislation, can save lives, but we knew there had to be another way. As Andrew Breitbart famously said, "Politics is downstream from culture." So rather than changing laws and hoping that minds and hearts would follow, Emily and I decided we wanted to do something more personal with Let Them Live—something on a smaller scale that could have a greater impact on our society.

You already know what came next. A few months after the Heartbeat Bill was defeated in Michigan, I was up late one night and saw a woman's desperate plea for words to speak to her cousin, who was about to have an abortion. Looking back, I can't imagine anything less political than offering to pay a woman not to have an abortion. The twelve hundred and fifty dollars I offered to Debbie was used to meet many of the financial challenges she was facing, and it helped her to know she was not alone; there was someone who cared about her and her unborn child.

That late-night donation started Emily and me on a journey that changed Let Them Live from a political engine, small though it was, to an in-the-trenches, baby-saving operation that set politics aside. Pro-life, pro-choice, Republican, Democrat—we don't care. We ask people from every walk of life to join us in giving women a real choice when they are pregnant. We have no agenda, other than saving lives and empowering moms to stand on their own two feet so they can love and provide for their kids.

Of course, propaganda doesn't merely affect campaigns. It affects real people. A couple of years ago, our social media director at Let Them Live received a somewhat unusual direct message. Olivia was being driven to a local Planned Parenthood clinic to have an abortion, something she was being pressured into, and decided to reach out for help, right then and there. Olivia searched for "#abortion" on Instagram and came across one of our posts. She knew nothing about Let Them Live or what our organization did to save unborn babies and help their mamas. She only knew that we were against abortion.

Olivia was an aspiring musician living in Atlanta when she met Shad Moss, also known as the famous hip-hop artist Bow Wow. The two hit it off at a nightclub and ended up spending the night together. Soon after, Olivia discovered she was pregnant with Bow Wow's child. Shocked and scared, she let him know right away, hoping he would be there to support her and take responsibility for the child he helped to create. But that's not what happened.

Initially, Bow Wow said he'd support Olivia, whether she chose to keep the baby or have an abortion. But as her pregnancy progressed, he told her he wasn't sure he was even the father. He wavered back and forth. At times, he seemed to entertain the idea publicly, even giving voice to the possibility on his television show, *Growing Up Hip-Hop: Atlanta*. But Bow Wow kept his distance and repeatedly accused Olivia of being nothing more than a groupie looking to attach herself to his money and fame. Olivia was rightfully hurt by such accusations, and while she knew the baby boy growing in her womb was not planned, she refused to call him a mistake.

Because of Olivia's connection to show business, there was tremendous pressure placed upon her to terminate her pregnancy. Bow Wow told her to have an abortion; he assured her she was in no position to be a mother. Friends and members of Bow Wow's family repeated the sentiment. They told her it was the right thing to do in her situation. Olivia wanted to keep her son, however. She wanted to be an example for other

African American women who find themselves in similar situations.

One evening, a friend of Bow Wow's called Olivia and told her she would pick her up in the morning to take her to the doctor's office for a checkup. But once Olivia was in the car, this friend admitted she was really there to take her to Planned Parenthood for an abortion; an appointment had been made for her without her knowing. Though Olivia resisted, this friend of Bow Wow's insisted that it was no big deal—just a simple medical procedure to help someone in her position. Olivia wasn't having any of it. She asked to be dropped off and grabbed her phone. She stumbled upon Let Them Live and reached out to us for help.

After our social media director connected me with Olivia, I told her to find herself a safe, comfortable place to live. I let her know we would cover the deposit and the first month's rent. Then I explained how we do things at Let Them Live. I assured her we would be there to support her during and after her pregnancy. I let her know we'd help her come up with a plan to make her life as a new mom work for her.

We came up with a comprehensive plan. Olivia rose to the challenge, making life changes for her own good and the good of her son, Stone. Olivia was able to stand up to the pressure and the propaganda of her community and her industry. But not everyone is. Every day, thousands of women believe the lie that abortion is no big deal, that their pregnancy is just a problem to solve, that the baby inside of them is just a growth to be removed, like a tumor. Holding baby Stone in her arms, Olivia now knows, beyond a shadow of a doubt, that the forced arguments of the pro-abortion culture are nonsense— and they can do a lot of harm, not only to the baby but to the mother as well. A life of regret is not an easy road to walk.

Olivia's story will touch many people, simply because she is in the spotlight a bit more often than the rest of us. But you don't have to be connected to a celebrity or have a career in the entertainment industry to influence people. Sociologists say that the average person will impact about ten thousand people over the course of their lifetime. At Let Them Live, we're changing lives one—or really two—at a time. As of this writing, we've saved nearly six hundred babies from abortion. If every one of their six hundred mothers will influence ten thousand people over the course of their lives, that means there are potentially six million people who will be touched by their stories and their courage, six million people who will now know about the goodness and joy that came from an unwanted pregnancy, six million people who will think differently when they hear the same tired arguments from the abortion industry.

And we're just getting started. Though Emily and I are no longer focused on changing laws, we are convinced we are slowly but surely changing the culture.

I have no regrets about our political activism in the early days of Let Them Live. Even though Ireland's Eighth Amendment was ultimately repealed, I'd like to think we challenged more than a few people to think clearly about issues of life. That's important, because now that abortion is the law of the land in Ireland, pro-life warriors are needed more than ever. And while the Heartbeat Petition in Michigan did not gain enough momentum to become law, our efforts did inspire pro-life groups in other states to pass similar laws. In Mississippi, for example, a law banning abortions after fifteen weeks of pregnancy was passed and later challenged in court. Eventually *Dobbs v. Jackson Women's Health Organization* made it all the way to the Supreme Court of the United States. In the summer of 2022, the Court handed down its six-to-three majority opinion, penned by Justice Alito, holding that, "*Roe* was egregiously wrong from the start. Its reasoning was exceptionally weak, and the decision has had damaging consequences" (*Dobbs*, 597 U.S. 2228, 2243 (2022)). In the landmark decision, *Roe v. Wade* was overturned, which triggered pro-life, anti-abortion laws in several states. Thousands of babies across the country are now safe as a result.

Political battles are important, and there are many more that must be waged now that abortion is an issue that must be challenged at the state level. But I believe the future will be decided by changed hearts, and the culture will be transformed by people whose lives have been touched by love. Propaganda is a powerful thing, but it's nothing compared to hundreds—and one day, thousands—of moms who have been able to hold in their arms a precious child that abortion activists sought to destroy.

CHAPTER 4

LESSONS LEARNED

I've never been afraid to stand up for what's right. I think that's probably why I was drawn to conservative social action in the first place. While I'm certainly not alone in my convictions, I am willing to take risks and follow the road less traveled, while most other people play it safe.

Take, for example, the time I was arrested—well, one of the times I was arrested. It was a few years ago, prior to the launch of Let Them Live, while I was completing a semester-long stint with the Leadership Institute. I was working with Young Americans for Liberty on the campus of Kellogg Community College in Battle Creek, Michigan. Our mission was simple: to promote the rights guaranteed to all Americans in the Constitution.

One day, we might blow up an eight-foot beach ball and hand out Sharpies; then we'd invite students to write whatever they wanted on the ball—total freedom to say whatever came to mind. It was a fun way to illustrate the First Amendment. On another day, we might dress up in orange jumpsuits and pretend to be escaped convicts. We'd hold up signs that read "I Support Gun-Free Zones" as a way of demonstrating the importance of the Second Amendment. Or I might give a short talk to students on our basic freedoms. It was a lot of fun, even if I wasn't always well received.

Do you know what got me arrested though? It wasn't some dangerous stunt or an act of vandalism committed to prove a point. I was arrested for inviting college students to learn more about their fundamental freedoms. Yup. That was it. I was placed in handcuffs, read my rights, and escorted off campus in a squad car for handing out pocket-size copies of the U.S. Constitution.

The irony wasn't lost on me. I was expressing my freedom of speech by telling other people about their essential freedoms, including their freedom of speech, and as a consequence, was denied my rights. You see, KCC had implemented "free speech zones," small pockets on campus where free speech is allowed. What that meant was that outside of those small areas, freedom of speech was prohibited, all in the name of not offending others. The whole thing is insane—as though a person's basic rights can be muted by stepping across an invisible line. Most people would consider any day punctuated by an arrest to be a bad day, but not me. Having an arrest record just energized me all the more. It made me see, in an undeniable way, just how important it is for me to stand tall for the things I believe in.

I stayed on with the Leadership Institute for three semesters in total. If you're not familiar with the program, the institute is focused on training young conservatives for leadership geared toward social change. It's basically a breeding ground for conservative activists, many of whom go on to run for and hold public office or start successful conservative non-profits. Since 1973, they've trained more than two hundred and fifty thousand conservative activists, leaders, and students including James O'Keefe, founder of Project Veritas and Lila Rose, founder of Live Action.

Every year, more than twelve hundred students apply for a chance to go to Washington for ten days of training. Of those, only three hundred receive an interview, and of those three hundred, around fifty are invited to D.C. for the training. At the end of the training period, there are only thirty field representative positions to fill for the coming semester, so nearly half of those who received the training will go home not having made the cut.

The Leadership Institute is selective. I bring this up not to brag but to emphasize how committed I have always been to the conservative cause. Not only was I selected for a semester-long term as a field representative, but I was also invited to come back for two additional semesters, an honor very few people have received in the four decades the Leadership Institute has been training young conservatives.

It was during the third semester serving as a Leadership Institute field representative that I met Emily. There was an undeniable connection between us almost immediately. In less than a year, we were married. Together, we were somehow more committed to the conservative cause, especially the pro-life movement. Saving the unborn became our mission; though if I'm being completely honest, I have to admit that Emily led the way.

About a year after serving with the Leadership Institute, a friend we met during that third semester reached out to Emily and me. His name was Jason, and he had heard about the work we were doing through Let Them Live. He wanted us to meet Nina, a single woman living in New York City who was facing an unwanted pregnancy. Jason wondered if we could help her.

We reached out to Nina to see how we could support her —to help her choose life instead of an abortion. Unlike many of the mothers we've worked with, Nina genuinely did not want to be a mother. She had fallen on some difficult times financially, but a lack of cash flow wasn't the only reason Nina was considering an abortion.

Nina was a Harvard graduate and had moved to New York for a career in journalism. By all accounts, she seemed poised for success. But then she lost her job, and shortly thereafter found out she was pregnant, despite having used birth control. When we spoke with Nina, she was on the verge of losing her apartment. The baby's father had abandoned her and she felt completely alone. She told us she was scared and didn't want the responsibility of motherhood.

My heart went out to her. So did Emily's. Clearly, life hadn't gone the way she had hoped. But abortion wasn't the answer. Ending her child's life would only add to the weight she was carrying. But as I mentioned, Nina wasn't interested in becoming a mother, no matter what financial support we could offer. So, I asked her a simple question, "What about adoption?"

Emily and I had been married for eight months by this point. Though we had been trying to have a baby, albeit unsuccessfully, we were open to adopting a child who needed a home. We would gladly welcome Nina's baby into our family if she would continue with the pregnancy.

Nina thought about it and soon consented to the idea. She told us she didn't want to have an abortion; she just didn't want to become a mother. Adoption would allow her to save the baby's life and put off becoming a mother until she felt better prepared. Emily and I were overjoyed at the thought of becoming parents to this precious child.

Through Let Them Live, we raised money to help Nina stay in her apartment. We also provided funds for medical expenses and other financial needs that would arise over the next several months. But Emily and I needed to come up with the money needed for the legal process of adoption. We also needed to meet the requirements of the state to become adoptive parents. We quickly learned there was a minimum income requirement, and we also needed to have a house before the baby arrived.

Up until this point, Emily and I had lived a very mobile life. We traveled a lot and didn't have many material possessions. When we first got married, we lived in a fifth-wheel trailer that a storage client had abandoned at the Berning Trailer Sales property. Then, eight months later, we upgraded to an Airstream I had renovated. Trailer life suited us just fine —we simply weren't very interested in spending our time or money maintaining a house and a lawn and doing everything else that goes with owning real estate. And since we were often on the road for political campaigns and right-to-life measures, being able to take our home along with us worked out quite well. But if we were going to become a family of three, we needed to make some changes. We needed to earn more money, and we needed to buy a house.

At the time, our salaries combined left us about ten thousand dollars short of the minimum required to adopt a child. To buy a small house—something that cost around seventy thousand dollars—we'd need a fourteen-thousand-dollar down payment. Plus, there would be all the legal fees we'd need to pay to proceed with the adoption. One thing was certain: Emily and I needed to get to work. Emily worked as a consultant for the Right to Life of Northeast Indiana, while I helped manage the Tim Smith for Mayor of Fort Wayne campaign. Even with both of us working, I knew we needed to earn more—and the quickest way to do it was to refurbish and sell a few Airstream trailers. Though much depended on the condition of the trailer and the amount I'd need to pay for it, each trailer could earn me thousands of dollars. Plus, if I used my time wisely, I could work on several trailers at once. So, that was my plan. And it worked.

During the summer of 2019, we brought our combined income level up to a place where we could adopt Nina's baby once she delivered. We also scraped together a down payment for our new home—a hundred-year-old, three-bedroom house close to downtown Fort Wayne and about ten minutes from Berning Trailer Sales. Looking back on those Airstreams I flipped, I can now see that the money I made wasn't due solely to my hard work; something more was going on. I received offers for those trailers far above market price. Though some people might call it dumb luck, I believe God was providing for us, multiplying the work of my hands so that we'd have everything we'd need when the baby came.

Back in New York, Nina's pregnancy was progressing. An ultrasound revealed that the baby was a boy. Emily and I could barely contain our excitement. In a few months, we'd travel to New York for the delivery, and then we'd make the trip home with our son in tow. We'd already picked a name: Alexander.

But not all the news we received from Nina was good news. There were complications to her pregnancy because of her epilepsy. It wasn't an insurmountable problem; there were medications that could keep her and the baby healthy. They were, however, expensive. Nina agreed to pay half the cost if we'd cover the rest. Of course, we agreed. There were other bills Nina needed help with. We agreed to cover those as well.

Emily and I were eager parents-to-be; there was nothing we wouldn't do for Alexander or his birth mom.

Then the unthinkable happened. On September 27, 2019, we received a message from Nina. She had had a miscarriage at about twenty weeks. Emily and I were heartbroken. In an instant, our dreams were shattered. There would be no adoption, no baby. The home we had purchased wouldn't need a nursery remodel after all. We wouldn't get to be there for Alexander's birth. There would be no moment of joy when we held him for the first time. No homecoming for our extended family to welcome him into their lives. It's amazing how much life can change with just a single text message.

By this time, Emily and I had helped ten women and saved ten babies through Let Them Live. Sadly, I'd learned that sometimes a woman in crisis doesn't always tell the truth. Emily had this sinking suspicion that things with Nina hadn't quite been on the up-and-up. Several times, we had planned to fly to New York and meet with her, and each time something had come up that caused Nina to push back our time together. Coincidentally, she told us she'd had a miscarriage just a couple of days before we were to finally travel to see her.

This was news that rocked our world, and we had spent about fifteen thousand dollars of our own money toward the adoption. I didn't think it was too much to ask Nina for proof of the miscarriage. She obliged and provided me with a letter from the hospital confirming the date her miscarriage was discovered. I didn't want to believe Nina could lie to us in this way, but I needed to know for sure. I called the hospital, but of course with privacy laws being what they are, the woman I spoke with could neither confirm nor deny that Nina had miscarried. I explained that I had a letter from the hospital and wanted to know if it was authentic. They agreed to take a look, so I scanned it and sent it their way. A short time later, they called to tell me the letter was not authentic. I hung up the phone in disbelief.

I had seen the baby for myself on ultrasounds. I had been so proud to show the pictures to family and friends. But when I pulled the latest one up this time, something didn't seem quite right. It looked too generic, too perfect somehow. Could this beautiful picture of the baby—this picture of Alexander —be a lie too? I did a Google image search with the ultrasound, and sure enough, Nina had downloaded it from the web. It had never been a picture of her baby.

I could barely bring myself to explain to Emily what I'd discovered. I had no words to describe how I was feeling, and neither did she. We felt betrayed and used, but mostly we felt the pain of losing a child that had never really been ours.

Shortly thereafter, I confronted Nina about what I'd found. I needed to know if there was some logical explanation for it all. I tried to tell myself, *Maybe this is all just a big, colossal misunderstanding.* But Nina had no explanation, no excuse, no words to change the ugly truth we'd found. She owned it; without hesitation, she admitted that she had lied to us. She knew that if she told us there was no baby, the financial support would stop, she wouldn't be able to get the medication she needed, and she'd be facing eviction from her apartment again. The early ultrasounds she'd sent us were of a friend's baby, and the latest one—the one with the clearest image in utero—was indeed from the internet.

To this day, we don't know if Nina was ever actually pregnant. Near as we can tell, there was a time when she believed she was carrying a baby, but she had either received a false positive on a pregnancy test or she had miscarried early on. Knowing all that she would face if our financial assistance dried up, she lied to us and continued lying until it was no longer possible to keep the lies going. Then she tried to walk away from it all by telling us she had miscarried in the middle of her pregnancy.

Today, when I think about Nina and the baby we tried to adopt, I'm not angry. I'm not even upset. Mostly, I'm sad. Nina didn't set out to defraud anyone. She didn't plan on having complications with her pregnancy. She didn't scheme to induce a miscarriage or anything like that. She just took life as it came, and she was scared. She felt trapped by the economics of her situation, and in desperation she made a series of terrible choices that ended up hurting Emily and me, people she had just met who were trying to help her.

In some ways, I'm grateful to have gone through the experience with Nina. As an organization, Let Them Live now verifies all payments. We require regular ultrasounds from a partner pregnancy center we select. We require access to billing and medical records, and we make sure there is accountability on all fronts. We even schedule regular video calls with our moms to check in with them. When someone gives to a campaign or decides to pledge a monthly donation, we make sure every dollar supports the real needs of pregnant women and their unborn children. We're a better non-profit as a result.

I began this chapter by telling you that I almost had a career in social activism. Whether I would have remained behind the scenes or stepped out in front, I can't say. Honestly, that wouldn't have mattered much to me. I was focused on winning elections and changing policy. I wasn't afraid to work with people one-on-one, but my goal was always the big picture: steering this country toward conservative principles.

People say politics is a messy business. That's certainly

true. Anytime there is money to be raised, backroom deals to be had, or compromises to be made for the greater good, things are bound to get a little murky. But do you know what's really messy? Helping real people, one at a time, in the hard and broken places of life. Things don't always go as planned. Promises are broken. Sometimes, people get hurt. It's risky to say the least.

With Nina, we felt the sting of risk, not just as the leaders of Let Them Live but as hopeful parents. We didn't just lose money; we lost a son. But that's the way love works. Love, in its truest and most beautiful form, risks for the good of another person. Love demands that we care for others the way we'd like to be cared for, but there's no guarantee that the love we give will come back to us. In that, love is always a gift. It's always offered with an open hand.

Emily and I are determined not to let our love be dulled by people who hurt us, whether the pain they cause is intentional or not. We have chosen to step into the messiness of loving people we've just met. In many cases, the women we help have lives that are very different from our own. Even then, however, we discover that at the core, we share the same need to be loved. Yes, there are real financial needs that make abortion appear to be the only viable choice for many of these women, but I've become convinced that money isn't the only thing they need. They also desire to know someone cares; they want to know that someone will stop and help them in their hour of pain.

Love speaks louder than public policy. It speaks louder than campaign rallies and political stunts. It speaks louder than the law or the courts. Love will change the world, one person—and one life—at a time.

CHAPTER 5

LOVE AND LOSS

The GPS on my phone said the trip would take just over twelve hours, but as I neared my destination, it only felt like I'd been in the car a few minutes. Time does funny things when you're falling in love.

I had met Emily a couple of months earlier at the Leadership Institute's summer training intensive. There was just something about her. We clicked right away. Though we started out as friends, we soon discovered we had the same energy, the same sense of humor, the same drive. We liked spending time together, and so we did—that is, until our semester assignments sent us to different states.

I was working on a college campus in Indiana, and Emily had been given an assignment a couple of hours from Boston. Hundreds of miles apart, our phones became our tether. We weren't dating—not yet, anyway. There had been no commitments made, no romantic declarations. We were simply wrapped up in the joy of knowing one another. We loved talking so much that it wasn't unusual for us to be on the phone late into the night.

One night, or rather, very early one morning, in mid-

September of 2017, we were wrapping up a long phone call. I joked, "I have to get going. I've got a date, and I've got to take a shower to get ready for it." Of course, it was three o'clock in the morning by that point; I wasn't planning on going anywhere.

Emily responded, "Oh—are you asking me out on a date?"

I played along. "Yeah, what are you doing tomorrow night at seven?" I had a crazy idea, and I had to give myself enough time to pull it off.

"I'm free," she said.

"Great. Let's have a video date. I'll have food delivered to your door. We can eat together and talk." Emily loved the idea. Meanwhile, I was clicking away at my computer, trying to see how long it would take me to drive from Fort Wayne, Indiana, to Webster, Massachusetts. I was going to have to drive through the night and into the next day if I was going to arrive at her doorstep by dinnertime. A short while after hanging up the phone, my bags were packed, and I was driving my Fiat across the state line. I didn't need sleep; I was going to see Emily.

Somewhere along the Massachusetts Turnpike, I pulled off an exit and found a steakhouse. I explained my situation to the host and purchased two uncooked steaks, sides of mashed potatoes and asparagus, and for good measure, a large house salad. After all, I had promised Emily a meal.

When I arrived at Emily's door, a few minutes before our scheduled video date, I played it straight. I rang the bell, and when she opened the door, I extended my arm with her delivery in hand. I had expected she would look at my face, realize it was me, perhaps do a double-take, and then invite me in. But she didn't. She simply took the food, said a polite thank-you, and shut the door. I laughed to myself, and then, through the door, I said, "Emily!" In that instant, she realized it was me standing there, ready to turn our video date into the real thing, complete with a home cooked meal. She dropped the food, screamed, "Nathan!" and came running back to the door with the surprise on her face still intact. She hugged me for a solid minute.

That night was special, one we look back on now as the start of our love story. Emily doesn't even hold it against me that I brought her a steak, despite her being a vegetarian. (Thank goodness I also brought that large house salad!) Driving a quarter of the way across the country to see Emily was, for me, a step into a future I hoped we'd share together. A little more than a year later, we were married. Around that same time, we started Let Them Live. All at once, it seemed, we had discovered we were made for each other—and we were made to help those who can't help themselves.

As the old maxim goes, "When you marry a girl, you marry her family." I wasn't quite prepared for how Emily's family would react to me. From the start of our engagement, they treated me more like a thief than a son-in-law, as though my intention was to steal Emily from them rather than to marry her. When it came right down to it, though, I just wasn't the sort of guy they'd imagined their daughter would bring home.

I recall the first time Emily and I traveled to Colorado to spend time with her parents and brother. Our first morning there, I woke up at about ten o'clock. I had had trouble falling asleep the night before—not an uncommon occurrence for me—and so I slept in a little bit to catch up on the rest I'd lost. Though I learned to live with it long ago, I have something of a sleep disorder. But there was no grace from Emily's family. They branded me lazy.

As time went on, the judgmental spirit emanating from my in-laws only grew stronger. They criticized our weight, the food we ate, and where we lived. They also looked down on me because I didn't have a college degree. The criticisms just kept on coming, sometimes in whispers and comments to one another, and sometimes right to our faces. Before long, I noticed that I had begun to behave differently around Emily's family. To keep the peace, I bit my tongue. Neither Emily nor I said much to defend ourselves. In the process, I became self-conscious about everything I said or did around them. I was miserable.

It all came to a head in the winter of 2020. Emily's parents, Ron and Louise, and her brother, Luke, traveled to Fort Wayne to spend Christmas with us at our place. In previous years, we had flown to see them, but this year Emily and I decided we wanted to be home for Christmas. It was their turn to be out of town for the holidays.

Even at our house, though, the denigrating comments flowed. They didn't like Indiana; it wasn't as pretty as Colorado. They didn't like our neighborhood; it was too poor. They didn't like our neighbors; their skin was too dark. They didn't like our house; it was too small. And on it went.

Inside, I could feel the anger building, not just because they were insulting our home and our community, but because I knew how Emily had been treated growing up. For years, her brother crossed boundaries and acted inappropriately toward her. He was strangely possessive of her too. Sometimes—even in front of me—he would pick her up against her will and carry her around as if doing such a thing was just his way of having fun with her, though of course it was never fun for Emily. Luke would call his sister a whore and promiscuous and other such nonsense. He would even smack his sister on the back of her legs, leaving big, purple welts, and Ron and Louise would laugh it off. No matter how much Emily protested, Luke continued this behavior. As if that wasn't bad enough, her parents had done nothing about it. They had decided the best course of action was to pretend it wasn't a big deal. Emily's pain and embarrassment were just swept under the rug.

On the night before they were set to leave, we decided to go out to dinner. Emily and I were in pretty good spirits because we knew that the next morning, Ron, Louise, and Luke were going to get on a flight to Colorado, and all the stress and tension they had brought would leave with them. But as we were about to head to the restaurant, Louise said something that made me snap: "This has been so great. What if we bumped our flight back a few days or so? Then we could spend more time with you."

Without hesitation or emotion, I said, "No, absolutely not." Louise started crying. "How can you treat your mother-in-law like that?" she demanded.

I was shocked she didn't know the reason. I wondered how she could have possibly thought this visit had gone well. But then again, I had been very careful to be kind. I had tip-toed around sensitive issues, brushed off insults, and did my best to keep the peace. *Was she merely pretending she couldn't sense the tension?* The condescending tone in her voice assured me she knew exactly what she was doing. And so, again, without vacillating, I answered. This time, a potent cocktail of rage and frustration and love for my wife erupted from my lips: "Because you're a bitch. That's why."

Looking back, I probably should have come up with another way to tell Louise how I really felt, but in the moment, my emotions could not be filtered. I spoke the truth of my emotions without decoration or diplomacy. I just let it fly, and I didn't care about the consequences. Growing up, Louise and

Ron had failed to provide a safe home for Emily. They had failed to care for her heart. And now, they were complaining about everything. So, yeah, another few days at our house was out of the question.

After the words came out of my mouth, a few things happened: Louise's eyes welled up with tears, Ron scowled at me in disbelief, and Luke balled up his fists and lunged at me. I was in shock. I couldn't believe Luke was hitting me, so in self-defense, I punched him back. I reared back my right arm and punched him square in the face. I hit him hard, and it felt good.

The next thing I knew, Ron was pulling Luke off me. That's when I saw the blood racing down Luke's face from his nose. Since I'd gone this far, I figured I'd let it all come out: "You know what—you're a terrible brother! Get out of my house and never come back. I don't ever want to see your face again!" (I may have included some expletives, but they're not worth repeating here.) Luke ran off into the night and we haven't seen him since.

Ron and Louise went after their son, and while they were gone, I called the police. I let them know there had been an altercation and that my brother-in-law might do something stupid in response. I asked them to keep an eye on our house, as he wasn't welcome. I tossed the family's bags on our front stoop, locked the door, and then phoned Ron to let him know he could come by and get them. That was it. We were done with the visit.

That was a turning point in family relations, to say the least. But it made me think about our own family—Emily and me. We wanted to have children, and at this point we had been married for a few years without conceiving. I assumed I must be infertile. Of course, I had no medical test to back that up; it was just a fear I'd harbored since I was a young adult. As the months slipped by and no pregnancy came, I started to believe I was living the fulfillment of that fear. But there was something else that steered my heart toward thoughts of future children we might never have. A few hours before I punched Luke in the nose, he said something that got under my skin, no doubt adding to the rage that was bubbling beneath my calm exterior: "You're not a real man," he had said. "That's why you can't have children." I didn't need to take my masculinity cues from Luke; I knew that much. But the thought that Emily and I might not have children had me wondering if we should take some steps to figure out exactly what was going on.

A few months after our family Christmas disaster, we decided it was time. I still believed I was the infertile one, but Emily volunteered to be tested. Testing her fertility would answer more questions for us, and the results would be more definitive. Once we knew whether she could have children, it would narrow down our next steps. And so, on a spring day in 2021, I drove Emily to Parkview Regional Medical Center. This was the height of the COVID-19 pandemic, so I wasn't allowed to go into the examination room with her. I had to sit in the waiting room while Emily submitted to a dye test that would determine whether her fallopian tubes were blocked.

Those minutes felt like hours, but I was grateful to have my dad by my side for most of it. He's a surgeon at Parkview and happened to be working during the window of Emily's appointment, so he came and stayed by my side as long as he could. I wanted to be in the room with Emily, holding her hand the entire time, reassuring her that no matter what the results of the test were, we'd be alright—that we'd find a way to have children. And yet, as I waited, I felt the weight of our assumed infertility. I just knew her test would show the problem must lay somewhere with me, not her.

Dad had to get back to work, so it was just me sitting there when Emily came walking down the hallway toward the waiting room. Her body language told me nothing as I watched her come closer. She sat down in the chair next to me without a word. And then, all at once, as though her heart knew she was in a safe place, she crumbled. Tears began to slide down her face as she turned and buried herself in my chest. We had our answer, though it was the one we had both dreaded.

When you run a non-profit that aims to help save the unborn, it can take a toll on you. But when you've just found out you cannot have a baby, it can be utterly heartbreaking. Day in and day out, you're confronted with stories of mothers-to-be who would rather kill their miracle than take responsibility for the life they helped to create, all the while you must keep moving, knowing the same miracle is beyond your grasp.

In the weeks that followed her fertility test, I watched as Emily's bright spirit faded somewhat. She worked hard at whatever she did—that hadn't changed—but it was as though the work itself had become a blanket to shield her from her newly discovered reality. By this point, Let Them Live had grown so that the two of us couldn't handle the case load ourselves. We brought in counselors to help. In hindsight, this was a tremendous blessing, for I could see Emily's heart, which had once been so very tender toward the mothers we served, becoming jaded and calloused. Each case was a grim reminder of what she couldn't have. Each unborn baby was precious beyond measure, though their mothers were ready to toss them away. And with each one, Emily's pain only grew.

We talked about trying to adopt again. The experience

with Nina in New York City had left us bruised, but now that we knew for certain we couldn't have a child on our own, we began to wonder if, perhaps, it was time to try again.

As the summer wound down, an old friend came back into our lives, though in truth she had never actually left. Margaret, one of the mothers we had helped a few years earlier, was pregnant again. Life out in California had not gotten much easier for Margaret and Stephen. Margaret had burned through the money she'd earned when she came to stay with us in Indiana. She hadn't been able to find a steady job, and she and Stephen were bouncing from one friend's apartment to the next. The thought of having another baby to care for, another mouth to feed, another life to be responsible for—it all left Margaret feeling overwhelmed. And so, she did something she would later regret: she took an abortion pill, a medication designed to starve her unborn child and terminate his or her life.

But that wasn't the end. J. C., the same pro-life counselor who had first connected us with Margaret was able to reach her once again. She convinced her to take an abortion-reversal pill, medication that would counteract the first pill. If taken soon enough, the baby would be unharmed. Thankfully, it worked, and Margaret's pregnancy continued. She still didn't feel equipped to be a mother a second time, so I began talking with her and texting with her, assuring her that, just as we had been there for her when she had Stephen, we would be there for her with this new baby. But Margaret insisted. She told me she didn't think she could handle another baby, no matter how much support Let Them Live was able to raise. She wanted to know if Emily and I would consider adopting her child.

Of course, we would.

It seemed so simple, so right. Perhaps, we imagined, it was

meant to be. Margaret and Stephen were very special to us. We loved them, and we would do anything in our power to rescue this new baby coming into the world. At the same time, we longed for a baby of our own. We would love this child and give him or her everything Margaret feared she couldn't. Our hearts were immediately kindled with expectation and joy.

Emily and I invited Margaret to come back to Indiana. At this point, we had a second house that we were using as office space for Let Them Live. She and Stephen were welcome to stay there and regroup as she prepared to give birth. Margaret turned us down, though; she didn't want to leave California and be so far away from her father. She did take us up on another offer, however. We arranged for her to stay with Nathan, a Let Them Live donor who lived in her area.

A few weeks went by, and we began making plans for our new addition. Margaret found out she would be having a girl, and so we began to imagine life with a daughter. We also began laying the groundwork for the adoption proceedings—making sure everything in our lives was in order so that when our baby girl came into this world, we could welcome her into our home. But this sweet season was short-lived.

As you may have pieced together by now, Margaret can be unstable. She doesn't always follow through on her decisions, and sometimes commits to a course of action that she knows isn't in her best interest. So when she texted me to tell me she had changed her mind about the adoption—and even about keeping the baby—I was shocked but not entirely surprised. Margaret's living situation was in flux, and money was tight. Though we were supporting her through Let Them Live, the pressures of life as a single mom with one baby and another on the way were just too much for her to handle. She told me she regretted keeping Stephen, though I knew she couldn't possibly mean that—not deep down anyway. She told me she didn't want to think about giving birth again, only to give her daughter to us. But she also couldn't wrap her head around what it would take for her to care for the child herself.

Emily and I were sick about this situation. We wanted to adopt Margaret's baby, but more than anything, we wanted to make sure this little girl would live. I told Margaret I would see her tomorrow and then I bought a plane ticket to Sacramento. I planned on staying as long as it would take to convince Margaret not to throw her daughter's life away. I was prepared to put my own life on hold for months if that's what it took. I assured Margaret that, once again, she was not on her own. We would stand with her, come what may. I told her we loved her and Stephen and the little girl growing in her womb. After five days, her fears subsided to the point that she was able to think clearly, and, thank God, she chose life.

In March of 2022, Sabrina was born, healthy and happy. And once again, the instant Margaret held her newborn child in her arms, she knew she had made the right decision. Life wouldn't be easy, of course, but she knew Sabrina and Stephen were worth fighting for. Emily and I were—and still are—genuinely happy for Margaret. Though our relationship with her has had its share of ups and downs, we do love her and want the best for her. That said, this was now the second adoption that fell through for us, the second time we were almost parents, the second time we had given our hearts to a child who was not yet ours and never would be.

Mourning doesn't end simply because life demands you move on and get busy. But joy does return. When we started Let Them Live, we did so to bless others—unborn babies and their mothers—but we were about to find out just how much the work could bless us.

CHAPTER 6

PROVISION

There is more than one way to lose someone. There is, of course, death, the inevitable end of every one of our stories. It comes to us all but somehow manages to creep up unexpectedly. When death takes someone we love, there is a season of mourning, and the people around us know to give us space or condolences or the comfort of a warm meal. These things don't numb the pain, but they remind us we are not alone. They aid us in our grief, fortifying us in our weakness and lifting our faces up toward the light.

But there is another kind of loss, one that does not come with a memorial service or flowers or an obituary. This is the loss of a dream that never will be. In many ways, this sort of loss is more difficult to mourn. It's an unseen and personal loss, one that the world does not commemorate, so it is rarely accompanied by the comfort of friends and family. This was the loss Emily and I experienced when we received the results of her fertility test. When we knew, for certain, that we would not be able to have a biological child of our own. It was as though we suddenly found ourselves walking through the death of someone we had never met and would never know.

For me, the test results brought sadness but also clarity. As I mentioned, I'd long suspected I might be infertile, and so I had been thinking about adoption for some time. Adoption, in my mind, was never a second-best option—not in the least. Adoption has been a part of my story for most of my life. As I've mentioned, my younger sister, Lily, was adopted, and I love her the way I would a biological sister. She is family, plain and simple. No qualification. No asterisk. And the same would be true of any adopted son or daughter of mine—they would be my child, full stop. Knowing how beautiful adoption can be, I was ready to move in that direction. But Emily wasn't. Not just yet, anyway.

Three long months came and went while Emily grieved what would never be. At the same time, she was still mourning the loss of her family. But her grief wasn't the kind that causes life to stop; she kept working and meeting her responsibilities. To a casual observer, she seemed to be doing just fine. But those who were closest to her could see there was something wrong. Emily was deflated, emptied of her joy. The normal warmth in her eyes had faded, and there was a sharpness to her voice that hadn't been there before. She kept herself in check, not losing control even for a minute, but it was clear there were some heavy emotions pushing up beneath the surface.

I did what I could to support her, but I knew from the start I could not give her the peace she needed. It was during this time that we were introduced to Melanie, a single mom who was pregnant with her fourth child. Throughout her pregnancy, she wavered on whether she wanted to keep her child or have an abortion. Eventually, Melanie made the choice to abort, and so she went to the hospital to begin the multi-day procedure. Being more than twenty-two weeks along, Laminaria was inserted into her cervix to dilate it in preparation for the cruel surgery that would end her baby's life. But on the second day, shortly after receiving a second dose of Laminaria, she called the Let Them Live hotline.

The fact that she reached out to us again showed me there was at least a part of her that didn't want to go through with her abortion. She was having her doubts, and I reassured her that we would be there for her—that we could come up with a financial support package that would ease the burden she was feeling. But from the start of our conversations over text, I could tell she wasn't going to be easily convinced. The anxiety she was feeling manifested in fits of anger. One moment, it was clear she was feeling guilty, and her shame was released in waves of rage aimed at me and Let Them Live. The next moment, she seemed to be negotiating for all she could get as though she were taking part in a business transaction—all as her child's life hung in the balance.

At one point, Melanie insisted on twenty-five thousand dollars for a new car. While we could certainly find her a safe and reliable vehicle, that price point was a bit steep for what we were normally able to offer. Then, without missing a beat, she asked for a hundred thousand in cash. It was clear Melanie was holding her unborn child hostage. She knew we were committed to life, and she was willing to kill her baby if we didn't give her everything she was demanding. Frankly, I found the tactic disgusting, but I tried to give her the benefit of the doubt. Perhaps somewhere in her terrified state, she had convinced herself that if she made ridiculous demands and we turned her down, the abortion wouldn't be her fault; it would be ours. Maybe she was trying to assuage her guilt preemptively. Or maybe she really was willing to dangle her child over death's door to secure a tidy payday. To this day, I'm still not sure what was racing through Melanie's mind; I just knew we couldn't play the game she wanted us to play.

Emily couldn't stomach what she was hearing either. She was horrified by the situation. Melanie had a beautiful baby growing in her womb, and yet she was using this precious life as a bartering chip for a bit of money. Emily would have given anything to be pregnant—to feel the kicks of the baby at night as she tried to sleep, to count down the days until the due date, to prepare our home and our life for a son or daughter. It wasn't fair. It wasn't right. Emily had counseled broken and desperate women before. She knew that, in their pain, they sometimes did or said despicable things. Still, no matter how Emily tried to understand where Melanie was coming from, she just couldn't make the leap. She had to step away. I asked Hollie, one of our most trusted counselors, to take over the case.

Over the next few days, there was a bit more back-and-forth, and Hollie was able to convince Melanie to sign a new financial agreement. Still, the issue was hardly settled. At any point while the law allowed, Melanie could make an appointment and terminate her pregnancy along with the baby in her womb—a baby she had already named Gabriel. We decided to put some of the things we'd been talking about down on paper. We wanted Melanie to have the truth somewhere she could read it again and again, if need be. Our letter read, in part:

I need you to know that you are not alone in this. If you choose life, Let Them Live will help you, and your situation will change for the better. Our team, especially our amazing counselors, pour the entirety of their hearts and souls into this work. Here, you will find not only financial support, but community and love. . . I promise you will have the support you need to raise this baby. In the under three years LTL has existed, we have helped many hundreds of moms – women in similar situations to you, who initially felt that their future would be hopeless except with an abortion – and have watched, firsthand, our support radically transform their lives. . .

Let us also make no mistake about what is going to happen tomorrow if you go through with your abortion. You will be brought into a cold, sterile room and prepped for surgery. After prep, you will be anesthetized. As you lie unconscious (Gabriel will be conscious for the duration of the procedure), your cervix will be stretched open. Likely this will be done using thin rods called "dilators," to create enough room for long steel forceps to be inserted. These forceps are designed for gripping – namely, gripping the baby's skull so it can be manually crushed. Once Gabriel's skull has been sufficiently shattered so as to end his life, a suction tool will be used to suck the mangled fragments of his body out of your womb. Lastly, a sharp tool called a "curette" will be used to scrape remnants of his skin, bones, and organs from the walls of your uterus.

Thereafter you will awake and will be told the procedure went according to plan. And that will be a true statement. The plan tomorrow is to brutally end your baby's life, who is a precious gift from God.

None of this has to happen. You have the power to choose something better for Gabriel and for yourself.

Thankfully, in the end Melanie did finally step away from the edge and cancel her abortion. She now recognizes that her son, Gabriel, is more valuable than any lump sum of cash. (We, of course, did not honor Melanie's request for the hundred grand. Instead, we found a way to meet the specific needs she was facing, and Hollie helped her find her way back onto her feet after the baby came.)

~

You don't have to be a doctor to know there's something therapeutic about a long walk on the beach. The hush of the surf, the smell of saltwater wafting through the air, the fine grain of the sand giving way beneath your feet—just being at the shore has the power to wash away the messiness of life, at least for a little while. Emily and I have found that the beach offers the space we need to clear our heads, to release the stress we've bottled up, and to recharge for what's coming next. Staring out at the ocean also reminds us of the overwhelming love of God. It's a reminder that the Maker of all that beauty cares for us. Against that backdrop, nothing we're facing feels quite so terrible.

It was on the Atlantic coast of Florida—one of our favorite places in the world—walking along the shoreline with our three dogs in tow day after day, that Emily slowly regained the peace she had lost. She grieved the results of the fertility test, and she found a way through to the other side of her pain. She mourned the loss of her family—at least the way she had always related to her parents and her brother—and she discovered some boundaries are for the best. She also sensed God was showing her how our story fit into the work we were doing at Let Them Live.

Melanie's was one of the toughest cases we had faced as an organization, and so I wasn't surprised that Emily pulled back in the midst of it, especially given all that she was processing at the time. And yet, when it was all over, knowing that she had helped to save Gabriel, her spirit was somewhat renewed. She could sense God's calling on her life once again, as though she were stepping into it for the first time all over again. As the leaders of Let Them Live, she and I had been given this incredible mission to rescue babies who would otherwise be without hope. And so, Emily began to wonder if, perhaps, this roadblock of infertility had been placed in our way because we were meant to rescue a baby who would otherwise be without hope.

Given our prior experiences surrounding adoption, Emily was, understandably, hesitant at first. My family had suggested we try *in vitro* fertilization, but we could not get on board. Medically speaking, *in vitro* was a viable option for us—there was no reason Emily could not carry a baby to term—however, there is no way to attempt *in vitro* without creating "extra" embryos as part of the process. We just couldn't fathom the idea of leaving those tiny, unformed children—*our* children—to linger indefinitely.

But there was another option, one my mom had suggested: embryo adoption. She had heard about it while listening to the *Focus on the Family* radio program. Truth be told, because *in vitro* fertilization is such an expensive procedure, most of the embryos created remain frozen indefinitely. Little lives, newly created, are paused forever and are never given the opportunity to grow and mature and be born. But some couples choose to place their frozen embryos up for adoption. We could give life to one of these forgotten children and welcome them into our family.

At first, Emily didn't even want to consider the idea. She was still mourning the loss of the biological children she would never have; she just wasn't ready yet. But after some time had passed, she began doing her research and praying through her feelings on the subject, and she eventually changed her mind. She could give one of these embryos—

these snowflake babies, as they're sometimes called—the life he or she deserves.

As of this writing, we are in the middle of the adoption process. When we signed the paperwork, we opted for the agency's Open Hearts program, which let donors know we were willing (and would rejoice) to adopt an embryo that has the genetic markers for a disability or an embryo that has been waiting for decades to be adopted. As strange as it may sound, we may end up adopting embryos that have been frozen since before Emily was born.

As quickly as we'd like to get through the paperwork and the background checks and the legal proceedings and all the necessary groundwork for our embryo adoption, we've actually hit a snag. We'll have to complete another home study, because in October of 2021, we decided to purchase a home in Florida, in the same area we've found so much peace and refreshment. In fact, our new house is only a couple of blocks from the beach. Someday soon, God willing, it will be to this home that we bring our new son or daughter.

Oh—and there's one more beautiful thing that happened in the midst of all this life change. It turns out Emily has a sister she never knew. Jennifer discovered Emily while clicking away at Ancestry.com. It seems Emily's father, Ron, had a relationship with Jennifer's mother just after he graduated high school, years before he met Louise. Jennifer is Emily's half-sister—and she's amazing. She lives in Iowa with her husband, Eric, and their two children, Cole and Brookelynn. Emily's been out to visit half a dozen times in the last couple of years, and they've quickly become family—real family. Jennifer and Emily didn't grow up in the same household, but they are sisters, nonetheless.

As Emily and I watch the story of Let Them Live unfold, we can't help but see God's hand at work in the lives of the women and babies we serve. He may work through the generosity of donors, the love of our counselors, and our own stubborn desire to see every baby have a chance at life, but I'm convinced it is God working behind the scenes to provide for every need.

I've known that for a while now as far as it concerns the mothers who are helped by Let Them Live. But as I watched Emily move through a time of anger and grief into a season of wholeness and joy, I could see His hand at work in our personal lives, too. He's given us a new home, given Emily a new family, and I'm trusting that, before too long, He will give us the child we've longed to hold.

CHAPTER 7

PRO-LIFE EMILY

If you've ever shared a late-night meal with a good friend and talked about the important things of life—faith and love and death and the meaning of it all—you know there's a certain level of trust required for such a conversation. In many ways, writing a book feels a lot like talking with someone you care about over pancakes at two o'clock in the morning.

Because Emily and I both wanted this book to preserve the sacredness of one of those important conversations, it made sense for one of us to take the lead and be the main voice for our story. But make no mistake: this is *our* story. We have walked this road together, praying and strategizing and dreaming and doing whatever's been required of us along the way. We are partners in every sense of the word. Up until this point, though, it's my voice you've been hearing as you've been reading. But this is Emily's chapter, her turn to share her journey and a bit of what she's learned along the way.

There was never a time in my life when I wasn't pro-life. I guess growing up in a strong Catholic family, it was just a given that life begins at conception and abortion is wrong. So, I didn't really think about the issue much growing up, at least not in terms of the cultural debate that was raging all around me. But that doesn't mean I was apathetic either. Though I didn't quite understand what abortion really was, I was a true believer from a young age (and I wanted to do my part to save as many babies as possible).

It wasn't much of a stretch, then, when I began my junior year at Colorado State University and started looking for a pro-life group to join. I wanted to raise awareness of the issue on our campus. I wanted to talk to women outside of the local abortion clinics. I wanted to take a stand for what I believed in. When I attended my first Students for Life meeting, I suppose I wasn't all that surprised to find there were only five or six students in the club. College campuses are liberal places in general, and Colorado State is a fairly progressive institution. What I was surprised to find, however, was that the Students for Life group didn't actually do anything—I mean, other than pray together at one of the nearby Catholic churches.

I have nothing against prayer, of course. I love to pray, and I know how important prayer is. But I was disappointed to discover that my fellow pro-life students at CSU never organized events or participated in debates or did anything that might be considered activism. They never took a stand, never made their voices heard, and rarely left the church building. Needless to say, I was frustrated with the state of things.

So I spoke up.

I joined the group and started talking about how we needed to be a presence on campus. To change minds and hearts, we needed to be there, participating in the life of the school and making our point of view heard. I wasn't sure what I expected from the group. I suppose I thought they'd be excited to get out of the church for a change. But that wasn't what happened. Instead, they all quit.

Yes, I single-handedly destroyed the Colorado State University chapter of Students for Life. Like I said, there were only five or six people in the club to start with, but I managed to scare them all away. I don't think anyone was mad; they just weren't interested in becoming pro-life activists. They had been content to pray at church and occasionally outside of the Planned Parenthood building right next door, and they could see I wanted the group to be something more. And so, they handed me the reins and left me to it.

Suddenly, it was just me. I *was* Students for Life. I restarted the group from scratch, and within a few weeks, I had recruited enough students that we began holding our own events on campus. Early on, we held a tabling event exploring whether federal tax dollars should be rerouted from Planned Parenthood to federally qualified health centers. I remember, after the event, some pro-choice students came up to me and told me I had changed their minds on the issue. There was even a Planned Parenthood volunteer who said she was now in favor of routing money to federally qualified health centers. I knew, in that moment, I had found something. I don't know if I would have identified it as "my calling" at that point, but I loved fighting for the pro-life cause.

As president of our school's Students for Life chapter, I connected with David, a regional coordinator for the Leadership Institute. David, who's still a friend to this day, helped me grow our little group into one of the best and most effective college pro-life groups in the region. Within a few months, being a pro-life activist soon took hold of my identity. My work on campus made me a regular feature in the student newspaper. I became known as "Pro-Life Emily," and I didn't mind one bit.

I had gone to CSU for a biology degree, on route to veterinary school and then a career as a veterinarian. For as far back as I could remember, that had been all I had wanted to do. Veterinary medicine runs in my family; my grandpa was a vet until he retired, and my uncle is a vet too. And I love animals, and so I was going to be a veterinarian—that is, until I became consumed with the pro-life movement. Students for Life became, well, my life.

Instead of spending my time studying, I spent my time organizing events and raising awareness. By my senior year, my grade point average had dropped to getting-by status. It was hard to focus on biology when I was so captivated by my new mission in life. Instead of reading (all of) my assignments, I read books on apologetics, bioethics, and philosophy. I didn't know what exactly I would do for work once I graduated, but I knew I wanted to spend my career being a pro-life warrior. Needless to say, my parents were a bit concerned—and yet they supported me; they could see the determination in my eyes and hear the resolve in my voice.

I wanted to save as many unborn lives as I could, and I knew one of the ways to bring real change to the world was to convince my generation that life in the womb is precious and should be protected. I looked at my campus as a sort of mission field, believing that for every mind I changed, an untold number of babies would be rescued from the abortion clinic. To that end, I invited Josh Brahm from the Equal Rights Institute to give a lecture on campus. CSU had made grant money available to student groups for events like this one, and so I applied. I was shocked a few days later when I received an email from the administrators of the fund rejecting my application. They cited the subject matter as problematic: they told me in no uncertain terms that they didn't want a pro-life speaker on campus.

The Diversity Grant, as it was titled, was specifically designed to bring a variety of speakers to campus to expose students to different and competing ideas. On a campus that leaned far to the left, and with the vast majority of students and faculty parroting the same, tired pro-choice arguments, Josh Brahm's talk would have contained exactly that— different and competing ideas.

It was clear from the email I received that this decision wasn't about scheduling or procedures or funding; it was about the school's blatant opposition to the pro-life position. I knew that as a student in good standing and the president of a registered student group, I had the right to access Diversity Grant money for its stated purpose. So I did what any passionate college student whose First Amendment rights were being quashed would do. I sued the university.

To be completely honest, *I* didn't sue. Instead, I got in touch with the Alliance Defending Freedom, told them about what had happened, and they sued the school. Thankfully, the case never made it to court. ADF was able to settle the entire issue with a strongly worded letter. The email I had received from the administration had clearly revealed the inherent bias in their decision-making, and school officials knew they had no choice but to reverse their decision and grant my request for funding. Shortly after they did so, CSU dissolved the Diversity Grant. It had been nothing more than a slush fund to bring left-leaning speakers and events to campus. It seems that once I made it clear they'd have to use the money to bring actual diversity to campus life, school administrators and faculty were no longer interested.

The lawsuit received a lot of press coverage, and I learned a lot about speaking to the media and being in front of the camera. When I invited Josh Brahm to campus, I had intended to influence a few hundred college students; instead I had the opportunity to talk about the abortion issue to many, many more. All of this led to more attention and better funding for our Students for Life group. And that, in turn, led to more activism on campus and in the community. We even brought Alveda King to campus. By the end of my student career, our little group that, at one point, had just one member—me— was nationally-recognized as the Students for Life group of the year.

Since I knew I wanted to be a pro-life activist, after graduation I applied to work for the national offices of Students for Life. The move seemed like a natural next step, and to be honest, I assumed I would be a shoo-in. After all, I'd received national attention for my work in college, and my group was recognized as an outstanding example of what Students for Life could be on a liberal college campus. I interviewed over the phone one afternoon, and I got off the call feeling really good about my chances. The interviewer did everything but promise me the job.

Everything seemed to be falling into place. My parents were worried I wouldn't be able to find a job after graduation, but soon I'd be working for a national pro-life organization— or so I thought. A few days went by, and then a week, and then another. I finally called to find out the status of my application, and they told me that they had hired someone else for the position. I was devastated, and for the first time in a long time, I felt lost. I didn't have a clear path to follow. I worried I had made a huge mistake abandoning my studies. *What if I can't find work in the pro-life movement?*

Losing out on that job at Students for Life turned out to be the best thing that ever happened to me. With that door closed, I applied for the Leadership Institute, which is where I learned a lot about social action and how to start a movement. It's also where I met Nathan. But I'm getting ahead of myself...

As Nathan has already described, the Leadership Institute field representative program is very selective. That year, more than a thousand people applied, and only fifty-five were invited to Washington, D.C., for training. Because my pro-life initiatives at CSU had received so much attention, I was accepted into the training program that summer. Even so, I knew only fifteen of us would receive an actual job as a field representative for the following semester. I was determined to prove myself.

I met Nathan on Facebook long before I met him in person. Being an experienced Leadership Institute mentor, he reached out to all the incoming summer staff on social media. To be honest, all of us incoming trainees knew who Nathan was. He had become something of a legend, since he was in his third semester with the institute—an achievement very few attained—and because he had been arrested for handing out copies of the Constitution. I liked him immediately.

When the summer began, we were both in relationships with other people, and so there was nothing more than friendship between us. Even so, I loved Nathan's sense of humor, and I loved spending time with him. We just clicked, even if our relationship couldn't be anything more than platonic. But as the months rolled on, we both found ourselves single once again. We kept talking throughout the summer, spending time together here and there, and our relationship developed into something more—undefined, to be sure, but something more than a friendship.

My passion for conservative issues, especially the pro-life

cause, was evident to everyone at the Leadership Institute, and I was selected for a semester-long role as a field representative. Normally, newbies like me don't get to choose where they're sent, but I actually had a few regional coordinators fighting over me, so I was able to choose New England as my base of operations. I'd always wanted to spend some time in that part of the country, and I saw this first semester with the Leadership Institute as my chance.

Nathan went back to Indiana for the semester, so he was eight hundred miles away from the house where I was staying in southern Massachusetts. We kept talking, though, and our conversations stretched longer and longer. And then, one night, Nathan joked with me about having to get ready for our date the next evening. He was going to have food delivered to my door, and then we'd "meet" on our computer screens and eat together. It was a fun idea. But honestly, the more I thought about this virtual date, the more disappointed I became. This was Nathan—not some ordinary, average guy. I wanted him to make a grand gesture of some kind. So, as the next day unfolded and our "dinner date" drew near, I was a bit sad and disappointed about the whole thing. I kept telling myself it was unrealistic for me to expect Nathan to drive a quarter of the way across the country just to have dinner with me.

When the doorbell rang a few minutes before our scheduled video call, I opened the door and took the food from the Door Dash guy, thanked him with a fake smile, and started my retreat into the kitchen. Then I heard him say, "Emily!" I sprinted back to the door and opened it. There was Nathan. I reached across the threshold and gave him a big hug. This time, the smile on my face was an honest one. I was so glad to see him. I was shocked but so happy that he had done something so sweet and beautiful like this for me. He had left his house at four in the morning and drove throughout the day to make it to my house by dinner time. He'd even managed to stop off and pick us up steak for dinner. (He didn't yet know I was a vegetarian, but it's the thought that counts. I ate his mashed potatoes and a salad.)

That night after dinner, Nathan and I walked around the lake by my house, Lake Chargoggagoggmanchauggagog-gchaubunagungamaugg. Yes, that's really what it's called; it's a small body of water, but it's somewhat famous for its ridiculously long name. Anyway, we held hands, and we talked. We kissed for the first time. And that night, I knew Nathan was the one for me. I didn't say anything yet, but I knew.

A couple of days later, Nathan headed back to Indiana, and I drove out to Western Massachusetts to help some college students with a social action campaign. On the drive home, I got a call from Nathan.

"Do you want to meet my family?" he asked.

"What do you mean?" was all I could say.

"I booked you a flight to Chicago. I'll pick you up from there."

It was another big gesture, and I loved it. But because I was still on the road, a couple of hours from home, I would need to keep driving straight to Boston if I wanted to make my flight. I didn't have time to stop off at the house and pack.

When I arrived in Chicago, it was late at night—sometime after ten o'clock or so—and since it's a three-hour drive to Nathan's parents' house in Fort Wayne, we didn't get in until the wee hours of the morning, long after everyone had gone to bed. Nathan showed me to the room in the finished basement where I would be sleeping, and we said good night. But as I lay there in the darkness, thinking about the crazy day I'd had, I began to wonder, *Do Nathan's parents even know I'm here? Did he tell them I was coming?* A few hours later, I got my answer.

I walked upstairs in the morning, and I was greeted by the shocked faces of Nathan's mom, dad, brother, and sister. There I was, this strange girl with tattoos on her arms and a piercing in her lip, emerging from the guest room in the clothes I had worn the day before—and they had no idea I was going to be there. Nathan didn't tell them, though I don't think it was for the shock factor; he just doesn't think that way. He wanted me to meet his family, and so he simply arranged it. He wasn't looking to have a conversation about it or get permission; he just wanted it to happen. I love that about Nathan. When he's passionate about something, he gives it his everything. That hasn't changed.

During my time in Indiana, I got to know Nathan's family a bit, and they got to know me beyond my tattoos and piercings. (Oh—and Nathan took me shopping, so I had more than one set of dirty clothes to wear.) The whole trip was really very sweet. But the best part was being with Nathan. When I arrived home in Massachusetts at the end of this whirlwind visit, it felt like I had left something behind in the Midwest. I missed him so much.

A year later, Nathan and I were getting ready to be married. Ten days before our wedding, I was having serious doubts— not about Nathan but about my career. I was still Pro-Life Emily, but I wasn't seeing a path to make saving the unborn my life's work. I'm a competitive person, so during my time at the Leadership Institute, I formed more campus groups than just about anyone else. But those field representative positions don't last forever, and now I needed a new job.

My mom was worried too. I had my degree but no career path. She wanted me to consider what it might look like for me to continue my education and become a veterinarian or a doctor. I started to think maybe she was right; maybe this pro-life passion of mine could become a side gig or a hobby. And so, a week and a half before the wedding, I took the MCAT Exam. I thought maybe I'd become a doctor and save lives that way.

This was the struggle going on inside of me. God seemed to be pushing me to devote my life to the pro-life cause. In that sense, my direction seemed clear, and yet I couldn't quite imagine what that path might look like. It was during these days of doubt and confusion that I picked up a book of inspirational quotes Nathan's dad had received for his birthday. I was thumbing through it when my eyes fixed on a verse from the Bible that seemed to jump right off the page: "Perhaps you were born for such a time as this?" (Esther 4:14).

For such a time as this. God had made Esther queen of the Persian Empire so that she would be in a position to help rescue the Jewish people from an ancient holocaust. It was her time to act, her time to do what God had called her to do. I couldn't shake the feeling that this verse was also meant for me. I thought to myself, *God has placed me right where I am, at this moment in history, to help rescue the unborn from destruction.* It was my time to act.

A few weeks later, Nathan convinced me I should start a pro-life non-profit to support our activism, even though at the time we didn't know precisely what it would look like. I prayed about it, and I told God I would do whatever He wanted; I just didn't want to counsel pregnant women in crisis or fundraise. Looking back, I laugh to myself, because those are the two primary things Let Them Live does today! I told Nathan I was on board. I was open to whatever running a pro-life organization might look like, and I began thinking about a name. That would be the first step. Again, I prayed, and "Let Them Live" came to my mind almost immediately. Though it wasn't anything audible that I heard, I have no doubt that it was God speaking to me. Nathan checked to make sure the domain name letthemlive.org was available. It was, and just like that, we were on our way.

Deep down, I was excited—and nervous. I wondered if I was being foolish not taking "the safe route" and pursuing medical school. But then Nathan's dad told me something that helped me see things a bit more clearly. He's a doctor, so he knows that life well. He pulled me aside and said, "If you become a doctor, you can impact maybe ten thousand lives during your career. But if you run Let Them Live, you can impact millions."

Today, I'm convinced the safe route isn't always the best one. In fact, if we're going to change this world, we need lots more people who are willing to step out in faith, people who are willing to say, "I'm here, right now, in this place, for such a time as this."

There are days when I feel overwhelmed. There are days where the weight of all the needs we face seems like just too much. There are days when I just want to step away, maybe not forever but for a long season. But there are also days when I get a phone call telling me a mom has decided to let her baby live—and those days make it all worthwhile. Those are the days I remember why I became Pro-Life Emily in the first place.

CHAPTER 8

WHY I'M HERE

This is Nathan again. As you could probably tell reading the last chapter, Emily's passion is largely responsible for getting Let Them Live off the ground. I wish I could say I've always been just as passionate about the pro-life cause, but that wouldn't be true. God brought me to the place I am today on a somewhat more tangled trajectory . . .

There's a story in the Old Testament about a king named Josiah. Though he inherited the throne at the tender age of eight, he was one of Judah's greatest leaders. He wasn't a brilliant military strategist. He didn't excel in expanding trade or brokering treaties. He wasn't much of a statesman or a politician either. Josiah kept things simple. Early on, he decided that, as far as he knew how, he would obey the commandments of God.

While that strategy was simple, it certainly wasn't easy. The nation had been entrenched in sin and idolatry for so long that Josiah's reforms upset the very fabric of society. He tore down altars to false gods throughout the land and restored the temple to its original purpose—the worship of the true God. He called the people to repentance and reinstated the sacred festivals the nation had long neglected. And he did something else: "He desecrated Topheth, which was in the Valley of Ben Hinnom, so no one could use it to sacrifice their son or daughter in the fire to Molek" (2 Kings 23:10).

You may be wondering why I've pulled us down this rabbit trail into ancient, biblical history. You may also be wondering what Topheth is all about and who, exactly, this Molek character is. Follow me for just a bit longer, and I'll make things clear.

Topheth was a deep and wide fire pit set in a valley just outside of Jerusalem. Molek was a god of Ammon, one of Israel's neighbors, but for a good deal of Israel's history, he was welcomed and worshiped by God's people within the borders of the promised land. It was believed that Molek would bring prosperity, victory, and health to those who offered him a child. And so, the people of Judah would bring their babies to the edge of Topheth and toss them into the fire in an effort to please the dark god Molek.

I bring this up because what Josiah did in destroying Topheth—in saving the lives of countless babies—was holy work. He was acting as a servant of God, helping to assure that God's "will be done, on earth as it is in heaven" (Matthew 6:10). While we don't tear down altars to false gods at Let Them Live, we are saving babies from death. The women we meet who consider abortion aren't thinking about an unholy exchange with an Ammonite god, of course, but oftentimes they are hoping that by giving up their child they will escape poverty and take back control of their life. It's an unholy bargain none too different than the child sacrifice that was offered long ago at Topheth.

When Emily and I first started Let Them Live, we both knew we were doing good work—even holy work. I used to say I was "striving toward sainthood," though truth be told, I wasn't yet a Christian. To anyone looking in, my life's journey must have seemed like a twisted and broken path without a particular destination. I can attest that's the way it felt walking it. But in God's hands, nothing about my life thus far has been aimless. He has led me to the place He has called me—a place of holy work.

I don't know your story. I don't know whether you're a person of faith or if you've even thought much about the spiritual side of life. Maybe talking about God makes you somewhat uncomfortable. Or maybe not. No matter where you are on your own life's journey, please receive what follows for what it is: the story of how God found me and brought me home. It's my story, and I have no intention of imposing what I've discovered upon anyone. I'm sharing it with you simply because I have come to believe that our lives are all connected in one way or another, and we all have something that can benefit those we touch. As it turns out, God often uses ordinary people to change the world in extraordinary ways.

My journey to faith and the frontlines of the pro-life movement came by a long and winding road. Along the way, there were psychedelic drugs and a prominent presidential campaign, several out-of-body experiences, and a trip to county jail. I came through a bit battered and bruised from the mistakes I made, but mostly I'm grateful. I realize there are some people who trudge through decades more of life before finding the place they're supposed to be. I can honestly say I consider the life I'm living right now a gift from above. I couldn't have gotten here on my own, not if I'd tried in my own strength for a thousand years. But I'm getting ahead of myself...

Growing up, I didn't think much about God—that is to say, we attended mass at our Roman Catholic church on Sundays. And it was there that God and Jesus His Son remained—on Sundays. And that was fine with me. It was all I knew, and so I assumed that was how religion was supposed to work.

Around the age of twelve, though, I discovered that God might not be so distant after all. A friend invited me to his church's youth group. Scott Harris's church was non-denominational, and it was unlike anything I had experienced up till that point. Music, games, food, and a room full of teenagers. It was fun. But there was more to it than that. There was something about the way they spoke about God. They talked as though He was a part of their lives, like He was family— someone they talked with that morning over breakfast. Scott's dad was the pastor of the church, and so over the next couple of years we kept up an ongoing conversation about life and God and the Bible and all the questions I had.

By the time junior high was over, Scott and I had drifted apart. But I continued reading my Bible throughout high school and college, and while I probably would have said I believed in God, I didn't feel tethered to any one religion, and so I explored paths beyond Christianity. My uncle gave me a book on eastern spirituality and meditation called *Be Here Now* by Ram Dass, and I ate it up. I also read parts of the Quran and explored certain ancient Jewish texts. At Indiana University, I took a class on Hinduism and another on Tantric Buddhism. There wasn't a religious tradition I was afraid to look into. From what I could tell, all paths led to God in one way or another. I also wasn't afraid of seeking truth with the help of various drugs, including LSD.

One time in college, I dropped acid with some friends and had an especially bad trip. It's hard to describe in words, but I can tell you this: it felt like I had broken free from reality, and that was a very scary place to be. I became hyper-aware of everything and everyone around me. It felt like I could sense everyone's true intentions—or at least what I perceived to be their true intentions. What I was sensing wasn't good, and I quickly became upset. I needed a break. I needed to leave. Though it was a dumb thing to do, I left the house where we were staying and began wandering the streets of Bloomington. I walked and walked, and every street sign I saw told me the same thing. It was like I was trapped in an endless loop, never escaping and never finding my way home. Frankly, it was what I imagined hell might be like.

When I finally came back to myself, I took that trip as a message from God—and He was saying I needed to steer clear of psychedelic drugs. For a long time after that terrible trip, I was paranoid and anxious, so it wasn't difficult for me to want to change my ways. In fact, I decided that instead of expanding my senses through drugs, I'd try dulling them with alcohol. And so, I began partying. I began to drink a lot, and I turned to softer drugs.

I can't tell you what my goal was; I honestly don't think I had one. I was just looking to have a good time, and then when that good time was over, I was ready to look for another one, and then another one. To me, there didn't seem to be a valid reason to stop. I felt nearly indestructible, and so I kept pressing into the party scene—so much so that it all quickly became a blur.

One January night, however, I made the mistake of returning to my dorm room still visibly drunk. Police officers were waiting in the area, looking for students like me to stumble in. As I crossed the quad, not exactly walking in a straight line, they called out to me. I ignored them, and they yelled for me to stop. I quickened my clumsy pace but still didn't respond. Their shouts became more urgent, and I could see they were coming toward me. And so, I ran. But the ground was slick from ice and snow, and I slipped and fell. I was able to get back up, but by then I'd lost too much time and momentum. In a minute, they caught up to me and tackled me to the ground—not a difficult thing to do, given the state I was in—and then they restrained me, breathalyzed me, and put me in the back of their squad car. At the police station, I was charged with public intoxication.

A court date was set, and I decided I was going to fight the injustice, as I saw it. The cops who arrested me were essentially looking to turn students into criminals. I hadn't hurt anyone walking across campus in a stupor. I probably shouldn't have run from the police—in retrospect, that wasn't the best move—but the way I perceived things, the whole incident had been blown completely out of proportion. So, when the date arrived and it was my turn to speak, I laid out my case, attempting to put the police procedures on trial. The judge, of course, didn't fall for it, but he could see I was a young college student without a prior record, and he was lenient. He put me on a year's probation and told me to attend every single probation meeting. If I did, the incident would be scrubbed from my record as though it had never happened.

At the time, I couldn't see the grace that was being offered to me. I had the opportunity to gain a clean slate and start again, but it all seemed like such a hassle. I continued to drink, party, and get high—though after my arrest I was more careful not to get caught.

Eventually, I dropped out of school; but I didn't tell my

parents, and they continued to pay my rent. I was content to eat ramen noodles and do whatever felt good in the moment. I bought into the whole Timothy O'Leary, tune-in-and-drop-out thing. Unfortunately, I dropped out so much, I spaced on one of my probation meetings. I was home in Fort Wayne, visiting my parents for a few days, and I didn't think it would be a big deal to miss just one appointment. But it was a big deal. The judge who had granted me the probation in the first place was not happy. That's putting it mildly. He extended the probation terms an additional nine months and sentenced me to ten hours of community service. But worse than that, the conviction stuck to my permanent record. To this day, it shows up anytime someone runs a background check on me.

Today, I look back on the arrest and the judge's words with thankfulness. The experience helped me to see I am not invincible. My behavior could get out of control and hurt people, including myself. Still, the lesson didn't hit me all at once. For a while, I continued to party. In fact, since I had dropped out of college, I started hosting parties and concerts to make some money to live on. It worked like this: I'd get five hundred people to pay a five-dollar cover charge, then spend a few hundred on vodka and Kool-Aid to make an ample batch of jungle juice. As long as there was music and alcohol, people seemed to be happy. It was an easy gig, and there were always lots of folks looking to party on the weekend, so I never ran out of customers.

In those days, there was a texting service I'd use called Swiss List—it was basically a database of local parties that we could use to send out invites and let folks know where our next event would be held. I liked it so much, I connected with the service's founder and grew the user base to five thousand subscribers. And that got me thinking about how to take things to the next level. I decided I wanted to create a mobile app that could connect people to any activity—parties, yoga classes, book clubs, nature hikes. It would be a way for people with similar interests to come together locally. I thought of it as a next-level Facebook, designed not to keep people scrolling through a feed but getting out into the world. As some friends and I began to write code and design the app, which we eventually called BeeThere, I lost interest in partying and the entrepreneur in me began to take over.

Around the same time, I returned to my search for truth with greater intentionality. LSD had left me feeling untethered and out of control, and so I sought out a religious experience that would help me regain control. I turned to transcendental meditation.

I had heard that I could achieve enlightenment if I practiced meditation long enough. All I had to do was learn to focus my spiritual antenna, so to speak. If I focused long enough, I could close my eyes and see spiritual reality. So, I practiced, and I soon found myself on a different kind of trip, one afforded without the use of drugs. One time, I remember sitting in my room, staring at a burning candle with intense focus. Then, I closed my eyes and continued to concentrate on the flame. I could see it in my mind's eye, and then it morphed and changed into a ladder. In my spirit, I climbed the rungs, and soon I felt a buzzing sensation run through my body and heard a popping sound in my ears. And then, suddenly, I was free. I was floating several feet above my body, looking down on my unconscious form.

For months, I continued meditating, and I continued achieving out-of-body experiences. But hovering above yourself isn't exactly fun; it's scary. I feared what might happen if something woke me up before I returned. But still I kept at it because I wanted answers. I wanted to have a connection with the divine. And one night, while camping with some friends, it happened. Lying in my tent in complete darkness, I meditated as I had dozens of times before. And like before, there was the buzzing sensation, the sound of popping, and then I was flying above my tent—only this time it didn't stop there.

Several pops later, I found myself on a distant mountain, and I wasn't alone. There was an old man there. He was different from anyone I'd ever met in my life. I couldn't read him. I couldn't get a sense of him, whether he was a good person or a bad person. I had no inkling in either direction. He was just a blank slate, a presence unaffiliated, neither light nor darkness. At first, I assumed he must be evil, since I sensed no warmth in his disposition. But then I settled on him being an entity who must be above good and evil, someone special. In this state, I asked the old man a simple question: "What am I?"

He responded without a hint of surprise, as though he had been waiting for me to ask. "You are not what you think you are," he said, "but you will do great things."

That was it. That was all there was to my vision. Immediately after the old man spoke these words, I heard the pop-pop-pop again, bringing me back into my body, although this time it was louder, more of a cracking sound. And then I was in my tent again. It was still the middle of the night, but I was so startled by what I had just experienced, I burst through the zipper of the tent flap and began telling everyone else what had happened. They weren't impressed; they were annoyed that I had woken them up.

My mountaintop experience was incredible, but it also marked the end of my journey into transcendental meditation. As I said, the whole process scared me. I didn't know what would happen to me if I couldn't make it back to my body. I wondered how meditation was changing me. I didn't want to lose myself entirely; I had just wanted to find a bit of truth, and I'd done that, so I decided to stop meditating and focus on this reality instead.

I can't say that it was God on that mountain speaking to me, but I do know that God used the experience to draw me nearer to Him. You see, it gave me confidence to take risks and follow my gut, and my journey ultimately led me to a place of surrender. But there were still a few more steps I needed to take before I would reach that place.

My work on the BeeThere app continued. My business partners and I had met a developer named Paul Wong, and together he and I worked on the code and the user experience. We also began raising capital for our venture. I knew that if we were going to do this, we would need to do things right. We'd need a big launch and the support necessary to scale as we grew. Before long, we had investors lining up to help us make the new social network a reality.

Then Paul decided to move to Silicon Valley. That is, of course, the place you want to be if you're pioneering a tech startup, developing the next great app, or designing a new gadget that's sure to revolutionize the modern world. Since I was no longer a student and wanted to press forward with the BeeThere app, I decided to join him.

Soon, I found myself living at the Facebook house, the fabled incubator of tech dreams and digital imaginations. While there, I met Steve Wozniak, cofounder of Apple, and became Facebook friends with other successful tech entrepreneurs, including Palmer Luckey, the founder of Oculus VR. For a year, Paul and I worked on the app, I raised funding, and I brushed elbows with famous and infamous tech icons. I was learning a ton about the technology industry, venture capital, and entrepreneurship. I thought I had found my place and my passion. But then, something happened I didn't expect.

On a nine-dollar fair from Spirit Airlines, I traveled home to Fort Wayne to see my family for a few days. While there, my dad had something to show me. It was Dr. Ben Carson's announcement that he was making a run for the presidency. I know—it seems every four years there are dozens of presidential hopefuls clamoring for the coveted office. But Dr. Carson was different. You see, in our house, we talked about him almost like he was family. Dad had long been an admirer of Ben Carson. He read his autobiography *Gifted Hands* when it first came out in 1991 and was so inspired by what he read that he decided to follow his dreams and enroll in medical school. My father became a surgeon because of Dr. Carson's example. So, in a sense, I grew up with Dr. Carson in the background of my life.

After we watched the campaign announcement, I had tears in my eyes. Then Dad showed me another video of Dr. Carson. This time, it was his 2013 speech at the National Prayer Breakfast. I was taken by it. I watched him, surrounded by members of Congress, the President, and other Washington dignitaries. I could tell he wasn't like anyone else in the room. He was a man of conviction, a man who cared about other people and who loved his country, a man who didn't play political games but instead spoke from his heart. He wasn't a career politician, and he wasn't looking for his shot at fame. Dr. Carson spoke what he believed without the typical veneer of political double-speak. He was different—and I was on board. That day, I wrote to the campaign and told them I wanted to help Dr. Carson get elected president.

At that moment, I decided I was done with Silicon Valley. It had been a great experience, but I was ready for something more. I wanted a life that was about more than organizing events and making money. I wanted to help my country. I wanted to make a real difference in the world. So I called the team and told them I would be stepping away for a short while. At the time, I didn't know I would never again work on the app with the same level of energy and enthusiasm. Dr. Carson's campaign needed help, and I was headed to Washington.

~

Within a few minutes, I knew I didn't fit in. Though it was only my first day as a member of Dr. Carson's campaign staff, the "Coexist" sticker on my laptop gave me away. I could feel every eye in the room staring at me.

Truth be told, I wasn't really much of a conservative at the time. On most issues, I was more of a left-leaning libertarian. I believed in the Constitution, of course—freedom of speech and the right to bear arms and all that—but mostly I just wanted everyone to be free to do whatever they wanted to do. "Live and let live," I would say. On the issue of abortion, I would have called myself pro-life if pressed, not that I had given it much thought. As far as I was concerned, it was none of my business what a woman chose to do with her pregnancy.

I was there to help with the Carson campaign simply because I respected Dr. Carson and believed he would make a great president. I didn't have to agree with all his positions. I wasn't there to stuff envelopes or make phone calls, however. I had come to help with social media and tech. I reported directly to the campaign manager, and I had access to the highest levels of data in the organization. Very quickly, I became part of the campaign's inner circle. With a background in tech and app development, I was tasked with sending millions of texts and helping the campaign answer hundreds of thousands of questions from voters quickly and true to Dr. Carson's vision.

My solution was called AskBen, a backend app that our team of twenty-five volunteers could use to respond to thousands of text messages every hour. Because the Carson campaign was so well-funded, there were no limitations on what I could do. If I needed something as I worked on the app, I got it. If I needed more staff or volunteers, I got them. It was as simple as that. It was a wonderful environment to work in.

AskBen was a great success, and for a while, so was the campaign. Dr. Carson was polling in the top spot. Being an outsider to Washington and not a career politician, he was exceeding all expectations—that is, until another outsider stole his thunder. From the moment Donald Trump entered the race, he took center stage. He was a wildcard. No one knew what he would say or do at any moment. And before long, he was leading the GOP pack.

Before Dr. Carson decided to step aside, however, I had the opportunity to ride with him in the motorcade on the way to a campaign event. He saw my "Coexist" sticker, blazing from the lid of my laptop, and we started talking. He asked me what that sticker was all about. I told him I believed in peace, not war. Thinking back on it now, it seems silly. Of course, I wanted peace. Everyone does. The real question is, *Is there ever a time for war?* Dr. Carson, in all his wisdom, spent the entire car ride explaining just war theory to me. He argued that, sometimes, war is the best option when overwhelming evil bares its teeth. Holding on to "peace" in those situations only facilitates more evil and harms more innocent people.

Though I'm sure he must have had more important things to do during that thirty-minute drive, he took the time to share a bit of his wisdom with a twenty-something kid who didn't have much of a clue about how the world worked. For that, I'll be forever grateful; it was that campaign, and that car ride in particular, that changed my trajectory. Dr. Carson taught me how to think like a conservative. He showed me that ideas have consequences, so it's crucial that the ideas we promote are rooted in truth and goodness, not mere expediency. Most importantly, I learned what the pro-life movement was really all about—and I became convinced that abortion kills innocent children.

~

After the campaign ended, I applied to the Leadership Institute. For three semesters, I worked for the conservative cause, continuing what I had begun with Dr. Carson. It was there that I committed myself to social action, and it was there that I met Emily and fell in love. We got married a year later and, soon after, began Let Them Live.

As we settled into married life, I was still trying to figure out how to connect with God. I certainly believed in Him—or at least I wanted to—but I hadn't quite settled into any sort of living faith. Emily had grown up Catholic, and she was grounded in her faith. I envied that. We attended mass together, and I hoped that somewhere along the way things would click for me, but they never did. At the same time, I was asking a good friend lots of questions about his faith. I'd known Chris Irak for years, and he was a solid Christian. Looking back now, I can see how he had been intentional about planting seeds in my life.

One of my biggest hang-ups about Christianity had to do with Jesus. I believed Jesus lived and died on a cross, but I couldn't wrap my head around Him being God in the flesh. I didn't like the thought of Him being sinless. I wanted Him to be a simple carpenter. I wanted Joseph to be His biological dad. I wanted Him to be an ordinary guy who sometimes made mistakes. I just kept thinking, *If He's sinless, how am I ever going to live up to that? How can I relate to Someone who's never done anything wrong?* That was the biggest hurdle for me. That was the issue that kept me from becoming a Christian.

Chris didn't give up on me, though. We kept talking, and he kept answering my questions. And even though I wasn't ready to give my life to Jesus, I looked up to Chris. He had my total respect. The more we spent time together, the more I was intrigued by his faith—and the more I knew I wanted him to come work with us at Let Them Live. I was grateful the day he decided to join us.

In those days, the organization was growing so fast, it was proving hard to keep up. It turned out to be the most stressful season for several of our team members, and I wasn't immune to the pressure either. Every day, new moms in need were being referred to us, and I didn't want to turn a single one away. I was determined to raise whatever funding we needed to save as many babies as we could. In 2019, we raised just $200,000, and by 2021, our goal was $2.7 million. It was a completely audacious target, but I was convinced that we could do it. We *needed* to do it to serve all the moms who were coming to us seeking help.

With all the stress piling on my shoulders, I refused to listen to complaints or objections. Before long, I could sense key employees pulling away. Then, my good friends Bill and Bekah, who were responsible for fundraising, resigned. I can't say the news came without warning. Bill had told me that the long hours he was working had affected his health. He wasn't eating well, his blood pressure had become elevated, and he and Bekah simply weren't happy. When I told Bill we needed to raise $2.7 million dollars by year-end, he shook his head and told me there was no way we'd ever raise that kind of money—it was simply too much. Rather than encouraging him or helping him to catch the vision for what we were trying to do, I barked at him. I told him if he didn't think we could do it, then he should just leave. And he and Bekah did. Emily and I were forced to take over their responsibilities, multiplying our stress even more.

Then, our social media director quit. A few key directors gave their notice too. Emily and I soon found ourselves handling lots of the day-to-day operations all while the organization was growing exponentially. The moms kept coming, and we couldn't bear to turn anyone away, so we just took on more and more.

It felt as though everyone was abandoning us just when we needed them the most. And it was in the middle of this busy, stressful time that Emily took that fertility test that rocked our world. If you'll recall, it was also during this season that she was dealing with being newly estranged from her family. Depression clouded out Emily's hope, and there was nothing I could do. I tried to be strong—to be her rock in the storm—but even there I buckled.

One night, I fell to my knees and yelled at God. I wanted to know why He was allowing all this to happen to Emily. I told Him she deserved better. I told Him none of this was fair. Could He see we were doing His work at Let Them Live? Couldn't He see how much it hurt Emily to lose her family? Couldn't He see how much we wanted a child? For four hours, I yelled, and I sobbed, and I unloaded on the Maker of all things.

That night, I also talked to Chris Irak. I asked him why these things were happening and all at once—why God had allowed so much stress and disappointment to come crashing down on us. He told me He didn't know the reason, but He said that God often allows testing to come into our lives. "Think about it for a minute," he said. "The work you're doing through Let Them Live is helping hundreds of women and children, and if it keeps on going, it will help thousands, maybe millions, of mothers and their babies." I knew it was true, but in that season I had been tempted to walk away. "If you buckle now," Chris said, "think about all the lives that will be lost. Think about all the families that will be broken. Think about all the pain and regret these mothers will endure if they go through with their abortions." Chris was right. I knew I needed to stand. I needed to rise above the challenges I was facing. If I fell, so would Let Them Live.

A short time later, in August of 2021, I took some of our team to a CPAC event in Dallas, Texas. A trip that should have been a break from the day-to-day stress didn't provide the relief I was hoping for. Instead, I felt the weight of all the people counting on me—our employees, the moms who felt they had no other place to turn, and of course the babies whose lives were being held in the balance. Late one night, I fell to my knees on the porch of our Airbnb. I was scared. I felt so powerless. For the first time in a long time, I knew I needed help. I needed power I didn't have.

I pulled out my phone and called Chris. Somehow, I knew he'd understand.

We ended up talking for hours. He encouraged me, and he talked to me about Jesus. He said, "It seems to me, Nathan, that suffering is inseparable from the human condition. Even Jesus—fully human, yet fully God—lived a life of trials and great suffering. Jesus willingly endured every pressure and stress known to man, to the point that His sweat became drops of blood. If even the Son of God Himself was called to persevere through such depths of suffering, why wouldn't you also be tested?" Then he told me, "I'm proud of you. You're doing the right thing. Think about the lives that will be saved through Let Them Live because you aren't giving up and you refuse to take the easy way out."

It was in that moment that I connected the dots. Let Them Live wasn't just a job or a cause; it was a calling. God had brought me down this path for a purpose, and I needed to trust Him with the organization, with my marriage, and with my life. I didn't have the strength to do it all on my own—not really, anyway. I couldn't carry all the demands and the stress and the uncertainties. Too much was at stake. I knew I needed Jesus to live in me and through me. I needed Him to carry the load.

I had thought the sinlessness of Jesus made Him untouchable. I didn't know how I could connect with someone so perfect. But now I knew that Jesus understood firsthand my weakness and my need. Right then and there, I committed my life to Him. He became my strength, my hope, my Savior. "Chris," I said. "I think—I think I'm a Christian now. I think I finally get it." We talked for a while longer, and I wept. Even though nothing about Let Them Live's caseload, Emily's depression, or the everyday pressures I faced had changed, I felt a great weight had been lifted from my shoulders. It was a turning point, the beginning of a new life.

I don't think I'll ever get over the joy I feel when I learn a mother has decided to keep her baby, but now I realize this joy is just an echo of the celebration in heaven. Ever since Dr. Carson taught me to think like a conservative, I've done what I could to save the unborn.

I came to Jesus with nothing to offer but a keen awareness of my need for Him, of my inability to do it all by myself. And that was more than enough for Him to begin transforming my life. "My grace is sufficient for you, for my power is made perfect in weakness" (2 Corinthians 12:9). Until I came to know Him, I didn't realize I had become a part of answering Jesus' prayer to make earth a bit more like heaven. But apparently, that's why I'm here.

CHAPTER 9

NO PERFECT CHOICES

There's a scenario that many ethicists and psychologists use to help people understand moral choices. It goes like this: There is a man who works for the railroad, and it's his job to operate the switch-track, which allows a coming train to go in one of two directions. Now, in this hypothetical, there is a small child playing on the railroad tracks around a bend, precisely where the train needs to go. He's too far to hear shouts of warning, and the curve around that mountain pass makes it unlikely he'll see the train bearing down on him until it's too late.

Most of us would say that the railroad worker has a moral obligation to use the switch-track lever to make sure the boy is safe. But there's a problem. If the worker directs the path of the train to avoid the boy, the train will take a pass still under construction and derail in a horrible wreck; most, if not all, of the two hundred people on board that passenger train will likely die as a result.

So, there that fabled railroad worker stands, hand at the switch, forced to choose between the death of an innocent boy and the deaths of two hundred souls oblivious to the danger they're in. What would you do if it were you? As it is in life, there is no perfect option in this scenario. Someone is going to die; there will be an earth-shattering loss no matter what the railroad worker chooses. But the greater loss of life should be avoided, and so the moral thing to do, as difficult as it would be, is to switch the tracks to save the train and its passengers, even though that means the young boy at play will most certainly die.

Like I said, there are no perfect choices in life.

What I'm learning as the head of a non-profit with a mission to save as many babies as possible is that I must often make difficult decisions—decisions that other people, without a view of both tracks, might question. Sometimes my choices mean we must stop doing something wonderful in one area to do something better in another. Sometimes, they mean I must disappoint certain people to help others. And sometimes, my choices have unexpected consequences.

If I'm honest, there are days when I feel like quitting. . . shutting down Let Them Live or handing the reins off to someone else and never looking back. Walking a road where lives hang in the balance, day in and day out, can be exhausting. Trying to help people who, at times, threaten to kill their unborn children if you don't comply with all their demands is stressful, to say the least.

At the same time, it's difficult to walk away from a mission that yields such beautiful and tangible results. There's something extremely fulfilling about hearing the stories of moms we helped choose life for their babies. Anyone who wants to know what sort of difference we're making in this world need only look at the photos of a precious one- or two-year-old being held tightly by the mama who loves them. It's a love like no other. That's what abortion steals. Planned Parenthood may promise freedom, but what they take is so much more valuable—and the freedom they provide is hardly free: it's more costly than any mom in their waiting room realizes. It's not an exaggeration to say Let Them Live saves women from a lifetime of pain and regret. We help them make the best decision they will ever make.

Our moms really are at the heart of all we do. Their stories illuminate our reason far better than anything we could say. That's why we proudly tell their stories on video, in social media, and in communications with our donors. It's also why, years ago, we created a Mom Advocate position at Let Them Live. At the time, it seemed like a wonderful way to provide meaningful work to some of the moms we helped get back on their feet. But just as important, it was a way for our donors to hear for themselves what a tremendous impact their dollars are making. Initially, I asked five moms to work part time for us. The job was simple. They could work from home and call their way through a list of donors, thanking them for their generosity and sharing how Let Them Live came alongside them when they needed support.

It all worked as I expected—that is, until a few months into this initiative when I sat down to look at the numbers a bit more closely. One of our moms, Diamond, had really taken to the new gig. She committed so many hours to Let Them Live, she was nearly full-time. She had also called almost all the donors on the list single-handedly. The other moms were putting in several hours each per week, but those hours were sporadic, and the number of calls didn't seem to correspond with the number of hours they were working. I realized that if Diamond had been working a forty-hour work week, she could have made all the calls by herself. Because she did such an amazing job talking with donors on the phone—she was sincere, enthusiastic, and professional in every conversation—it wouldn't be a bad thing if she were our one-and-only official Mom Advocate.

When I added up what it would cost us to bring Diamond on full-time and compared it to what we were currently paying five part-time Mom Advocates, I realized Let Them Live could save about six thousand dollars every month. That's seventy-two thousand dollars—and at least five babies saved from abortion—every year. You see, it costs Let Them Live an average of $13,944 to save a baby in the womb. Every mom's situation is different, of course, but most women who come to us need the same things in order to choose life: a stable place to live, reliable transportation, and necessities like diapers, a crib, and a stroller. Our payroll includes Mom Advocates like Diamond as well as full-time pregnancy counselors who give moms much-needed emotional support. By changing the Mom Advocate program, we'd be able to free up enough money to take on at least five more moms every year. I knew what we had to do.

I made the change. I talked to Bill and Bekah, our director of donor relations and our director of donor cultivation, respectively. I explained that, moving forward, Diamond would move into a full-time role, handling all our Mom Advocate needs; we would also be cutting the other four positions from the budget to save money. What I didn't know at the time was just how much Bill and Bekah hated that decision. They cared about every person on our staff, and they had a special place in their hearts for our Mom Advocates, since they had chosen life in direct response to Let Them Live's efforts. Of course, Emily and I both cared (and still care) deeply about everyone who partners with us at Let Them Live, especially the moms who not only choose life but also choose to join us in our mission. It was just that we could see the bigger picture, while Bill and Bekah saw, first and foremost, the disappointment that would wash over those we needed to let go.

One of the Mom Advocates we let go was Chandra. At the time, I didn't think letting her go would matter that much to her. She hadn't clocked any hours with us for at least a month. For all I knew, she had already decided the Mom Advocate position wasn't for her. The truth was, however, that Chandra had been struggling with severe depression and had been unable to work.

When Chandra was younger, she had been sexually abused. As a result, she had experienced more than one mental breakdown over the years. When we met her, she was on medication for anxiety and depression, which was helping her find mental and emotional equilibrium. The thing everyone remembers about her from that time is how sweet she was. She was already a single mom to a little boy named James, and she was pregnant with her second child. Her financial struggles made abortion appear to be the easy answer to her stress, but Chandra didn't want to kill her baby; she wanted to choose life. And so, when she contacted Let Them Live, we worked with her and provided a bit of financial stability so that she could welcome her new baby into the world. And that she did.

On November 3, 2020, Chandra gave birth to a beautiful baby girl she named Mary. Chandra told us that after she had James, she suffered from severe postpartum depression. As a result, she didn't bond with him immediately. In fact, she said it took her a few weeks to feel that she even loved her baby boy. As sad as that was, her connection to Mary was just the opposite; she loved her immediately. That's because the medication Chandra was taking had gotten her anxiety under control. But there was a severe side effect: little Mary was born addicted to the drug, and she suffered severe withdrawals when she stopped getting them from her mama. It broke Chandra's heart to watch her sweet little girl shaking and crying as she held her.

That would be a lot for any mom to handle, but Chandra was also financially insecure. Let Them Live walked with her through those first few months as a mom of two. We paid off her car and helped her with other expenses as she settled into her new normal. And it was only a few weeks following Mary's birth that we offered her the part-time job as a Mom Advocate. Chandra was elated. She had seen firsthand the difference our organization could make in the lives of women with unexpected pregnancies, and she wanted to give something back. This was a way to do just that while also providing for her family.

As I mentioned, the Mom Advocate role, as originally designed, was only part-time and was created to be a flexible, work-from-home job. That meant Chandra was free to log as many or as few hours as she wanted to, as long as she was trying her best. As the months went by, our team saw those hours dwindle and then disappear entirely. Then, she told Bekah she needed a few weeks off from making calls. She told her that she was struggling with suicidal thoughts. Her stress level was at an all-time high, and her anxiety had come back with a vengeance. Then, she simply stopped responding to Bekah's calls, texts, and emails.

We learned that Chandra had been dating someone new, and so we reached out to the new boyfriend, David, to make sure she was okay. David confirmed what we suspected: Chandra was in a bad place, and while he was doing everything he could to support her, he wasn't sure when or how she would pull out of it. Chandra's counselor Hollie asked David to pass along a message. "Please tell her we love her," she said. "We'd love to hear from her anytime she's able to call or text."

A few weeks later, Chandra reached out to Rebekah, our director of donor cultivation. She apologized for ghosting us. She sounded healthier, full of resolve and renewed vigor. It seemed, perhaps, Chandra was ready to begin working again. More importantly, it seemed she might be ready to open up to us again. But in the months that followed, Chandra did little to change things. She worked few, if any, hours from week to week, and she was difficult to get in touch with.

In July of 2021, nearly a year after she'd given birth to Mary, we finally learned what she had really been walking through during those silent months. During a phone call, Chandra broke down in tears. She apologized profusely for not responding to our calls and texts. She wanted to know if she was still considered a Let Them Live mom. We told her that, of course, she was. Even though the financial payments had stopped, we were still there to help her and support her if she needed something. Chandra, then, told us about past abuse she had experienced and her struggles with depression. We had known all of that, so it seemed she was rehearsing the sad details of her life's story as a way of introducing a new chapter, one equally difficult. She revealed David had been emotionally abusive and violent toward her, and she had endured several altercations that left her fearing for her safety. The last time, she told us, he threatened to rape her if she didn't treat him right.

Rebekah told Chandra she needed to call the police if she thought there was anything credible to David's threats. Through tears, she said she didn't really think he'd follow through with it. Even so, Rebekah encouraged her to be careful, and if she ever felt he might do something to harm her, she needed to call the police. I assured her that I, and everyone else at Let Them Live, was there to support her.

Obviously, that was a troubling conversation, the kind I hope our team would never have to have with any of our moms. But Rebekah meant what she said: if Chandra needed our help, we'd be there for her. As it turned out, she did need our help. Shortly after we reconnected with Chandra, she called to tell us she was pregnant again. She hadn't planned this pregnancy, of course. She knew David was not a safe person, and yet she was now pregnant with his child. We were ready to help her in any way we could.

Chandra wasn't the first Let Them Live mom to find herself in this situation, and we don't allocate resources based on a woman's choices or circumstances; we strive to help everyone that comes to us. In fact, that's why, around the same time Chandra told us she was pregnant, I decided to change the Mom Advocate program.

In hindsight, I can see how members of our staff and Chandra herself were hurt by the decision, but it wasn't personal. I was thinking only of the babies that might be saved if we reduced our payroll and made our outreach to donors more efficient. In fact, I had the same thought in mind when I revamped our gift card program. As you may recall, one of the ways we help moms when they first come to us is through gift cards. We'd provide cards for Wal-Mart, local grocery stores, gas stations, and the like. Quickly, they became part of a standard package we offered to all moms. After all, everyone needs to eat and put gas in their car. But when I ran the numbers, I saw that we were spending more than three-hundred thousand dollars per year on gift cards alone. After talking with Emily, I decided we needed to change tactics. We'd still have gift cards on hand for when they were needed, but we wouldn't hand them out automatically; we'd only give them out to meet specific needs.

As you can imagine, that decision was unpopular with our counselors. As they talked with moms in crisis, they could no longer offer a package of gift cards, no strings attached. We would, of course, still meet real needs. We'd pay the rent if that was a concern. We'd find reliable transportation if that was an issue. But we would no longer give every mom who came to us thousands of dollars in prepaid gift cards without there being a specific need to meet. Again, I just looked at the numbers and thought about how many more babies we could save. Three-hundred thousand dollars amounted to a lot of lives rescued—and that's what Let Them Live is all about.

At the time, I suspected I might receive some pushback about these money-saving decisions, but I had no idea how bad it would be. As I mentioned in a previous chapter, Bill and Bekah resigned from Let Them Live. I can't say these new policies were the only factor, but they certainly contributed to the burnout my longtime friends experienced around this time. There were other resignations as well. Lexi, our director of counseling quit, as did Hannah, who managed our fundraising department. It was a sad season, full of loss and confusion. To this day, the relationships I had with these former team members, many of which preceded our time together at Let Them Live, are fractured. All of them blocked Emily, me, and the other core members of the Let Them Live team on social media. There has been little offered in the way of explanation, only silence. To be honest, it still hurts.

What hurt more in those days, however, is what happened to Chandra. When she first told us she was pregnant again, our counselors reached out to her several times, trying to see how Let Them Live could come alongside her in her time of uncertainty and need, just as we had done with her previous pregnancy. After about a month of trying, however, Chandra stopped answering our texts and calls. She became completely non-responsive. She wanted nothing to do with me or the organization. I have to believe that was, at least in part, because we terminated her part-time job.

A few months later, we received word that Chandra had ended her pregnancy with an abortion. It hit our whole team really hard. Chandra's had been a wonderful success story, and her abortion an ugly reminder that our work is never done. Even a mom who has previously chosen life is not immune to the siren song of our culture of death. Truth be told, about 11 percent of the women we counsel do end up choosing abortion. No matter how many times it happens, though, it never gets any easier. It always feels like a punch in the gut. It's a loss that will only be realized in the light of eternity. Who knows what Chandra's little girl or boy might have become or how many lives they would have touched?

Chandra's baby wasn't the only victim of her decision. Chandra suffered too, and will probably feel the pain of her choice for the rest of her life. Nine months after her abortion, Chandra wrote to us. She said, "I guess I didn't realize how much I wanted the baby until it was too late. I'm so hurt, and I hate myself even more now." There is healing for women who have chosen abortion, and we directed Chandra to several resources that will help her step out from the shadow of guilt and shame. But of course, it won't be easy. It never is.

Our tagline at Let Them Live is "Defending the Defenseless." Every decision I make hinges on that idea. We're here to help those who can't help themselves. And so, while I feel terrible about Chandra's abortion and the loss of several valuable members of my team, I can't say I regret my decision to streamline our budget. Let Them Live is not a business. We don't deal in dollars and cents, profits and losses, or the value of our stock (we don't have any). We rescue the unborn. The financial side of our organization—donor gifts, fundraising campaigns, and operating expenses—all exist to serve the weakest members of our society. They are our number-one priority.

Years ago, when I agreed to pay a stranger twelve-hundred and fifty dollars to cancel her abortion appointment, I had to process what I was really doing. I was putting a price on the life of an unborn child. I know—it sounds cold. A baby's right to exist can't be measured in cash payments. There is no way to put a price on a human life. And yet, that's exactly what we must do. The "price" is the amount it takes for a mother to feel financially stable enough to keep her baby. And so, years into this experiment we call Let Them Live, my mind has trained itself to think about money in terms of lives that could be saved.

There are no perfect decisions, only good and beautiful outcomes. Those are what I'm striving for. That's why I get up every morning and wear as many different hats as I do to keep Let Them Live afloat. Our team is fighting to change the world. As with any revolution, there are some who won't understand what we're trying to do. There will be others who join us for a season and then go in a different direction after a while. And there will be some who are unwilling to sacrifice for the greater good. But there will also be those who catch our vision, roll up their sleeves, and join us. With every life saved and every story told, the culture of life takes new ground. So, I say, bring on the difficult decisions. There's a bright, new future waiting for those of us who can make the tough calls.

CHAPTER 10

THE FIRST FIVE HUNDRED ROADSTERS

Chances are, if you go out today and drive around town for more than a few minutes, you'll pass by a Tesla or two. These high-end electric vehicles have become so commonplace, it's hard to remember that in the early years, many analysts predicted Tesla Motors would flop. Electric vehicles with any sort of reasonable driving range were prohibitively expensive to produce, and previous attempts at environmentally sensitive vehicles had all the style of, well, a Toyota Prius.

But the founders of Tesla—Martin Eberhard and Marc Tarpenning—had a vision. They would start out catering to the wealthy. In due time, they'd introduce electric vehicles to the mass market, transforming the auto industry and changing the world. But they started with a roadster. They knew they couldn't produce a sleek roadster that could travel three hundred miles on a charge without giving it a high price tag, so they didn't try. They just created the coolest car imaginable—fast and beautiful with lots of driving range—and sold it to those who could afford it. When Elon Musk took over the company as CEO in 2008, he grabbed hold of this vision and made it happen. He set a goal of selling five hundred Roadsters at $98,000 a pop; then, once that mission was completed, he used that revenue to produce a proof of concept to raise the funds needed to produce the Model S, a mainstream BMW and Mercedes competitor, priced for a much larger market. And on it went. Musk scaled and scaled to bring prices down. Today, while Tesla vehicles are still not considered entry-level by any stretch of the imagination, the base Model 3 starts at $46,990, less than half of the Roadster's original sticker price.

I bring up Musk and the Tesla Roadster because it reminds me of what we're doing these days at Let Them Live. As Providence would have it, as of this writing, we saved our five hundredth baby from abortion just a few months ago. Those babies are a bit like Musk's Roadsters: the first five hundred proved our concept, and now we're ready to scale (and no, we will not be launching one into orbit, as Musk famously did with one of his cars). Our goal is to replicate our model of pro-life ministry far and wide so that anywhere there is a community of people who want to rescue the unborn and come alongside vulnerable moms, Let Them Live can provide a ready-to-serve model for fundraising and ministry.

Not too long ago, Emily had the opportunity to speak to a group of students at Stetson University in Central Florida. She told them about our work at Let Them Live, how we got started, and what we believe about life. While many of the folks who gathered to hear Emily tell her story were pro-life themselves, a large contingent of pro-choice students were there too. As I've discovered for myself over the years, this isn't uncommon. Pro-abortion activists frequently attend pro-life events and take seats at pro-life talks for no other reason than to be a voice of dissent and opposition.

While it can be disconcerting when you're the one up on the stage, I actually admire the passion of men and women who are vehemently committed to the pro-choice position. I once would have counted myself among them—and while I wouldn't have barked as loudly as they did, I wouldn't have objected to being regarded as a member of their pack. So, while my mind and heart have changed on the issue, I respect their devotion to their cause. They really do believe they are helping women by standing up for a woman's supposed right to an abortion. I know Emily shares the same respect, even if she never shared their beliefs. In fact, both of us wish we saw the same degree of passion in the pro-life community.

In her talk at Stetson, Emily reserved her greatest challenge for the pro-lifers who were there in the room. "It's easy enough to walk around and say, 'I'm pro-life,'" she told them, "but if we're ever going to provide any alternative to abortion, we've got to do something. We've got to put our money where our mouth is. And that's something that pro-choice people actually get right. They call pro-lifers out for not doing anything. And they should. We should be called out. We've got to do something. It's not enough to say you're pro-life."

Over the years, I've seen the pro-life community do some amazing things to reduce the number of abortions in this country. They've campaigned. They've picketed. They've counseled. They've marched. And they've been effective. *Roe v. Wade* was overturned in the summer of 2022. Who knows how many lives have been saved because of the work the pro-life community has done? But do you know what I think about when I think of most pro-life organizations? I think about what they're against.

In the simplest of terms, to be pro-life in this country is to be against abortion. It's to be against its legality, its funding, and its practice. To be pro-life should also mean being pro-baby, because when an abortion is stopped, a life is saved. But in reality, child and maternal well-being have been neglected by most pro-life activists. Most pro-life efforts do nothing to address the underlying issues that made abortion attractive to a mom in crisis in the first place, or help to create an environment where the new baby can thrive after being saved from the abortionist. Advocates for choice call this being "pro-birth" rather than "pro-life."

To be fair, there are pregnancy resource centers engaged in this effort, and I don't want to belittle their work. In fact, many of our most engaged partners in the field are pregnancy resource centers. What they do in their local communities is amazing, and greatly needed. But for every person who works for or supports a pregnancy resource center, there are a thousand men and women who consider themselves pro-life simply because they vote Republican and tell their friends they're opposed to abortion.

At Let Them Live, we're attempting to carve out a new path, one that people with pro-life *and* pro-choice convictions can travel together. We believe the best way to save the unborn is to support mothers in desperate situations—to give them another choice besides abortion. And we believe the way forward is to replicate our strategy far and wide. We want the Let Them Live approach to spread to every pro-life community across the country—and later, the world. There are too many moms in need, too many babies in danger, and too many pro-life advocates sitting on the sidelines, wondering what they can do to make an actual difference. It's just like Emily told those students: "We've got to do something. It's not enough to say you're pro-life."

Father Taylor Reynolds certainly wanted to do something. As the pastoral administrator for the Diocese of Alexandria in Central Louisiana, his churches have always been staunchly pro-life. But when *Roe v. Wade* was overturned and abortion was essentially outlawed in the state, he found himself with a flock in need of a new mission.

Father Reynolds understands that being pro-life means more than just stopping abortions; it means caring for people at every stage of life. And that's what he preaches and teaches. St. Joseph's in Marksville, one of two churches in Father Reynolds' care, was eager to look beyond their own community, to a city far away where abortion still claims the lives of innocent children every single day. That's where Let Them Live came into their story. Father Reynolds heard about our Adopt-a-Mom program and decided it was the perfect way for the faithful of St. Joseph's to love their neighbor, a neighbor no one in that congregation had ever met. That neighbor's name was Ana.

Our Adopt-a-Mom program is exactly what it sounds like. We connect a vulnerable mom in need of financial help with a community—a church, a pregnancy resource center, a Bible study, a student association, a neighborhood—and that community "adopts" the mom, providing everything she needs to prepare for the birth of her child. Usually, this involves local fundraisers over the remainder of the mom's pregnancy. And honestly, that's one of the things that makes the program so special. Fundraisers reflect the character of the community, and if they're done well, they involve just about everyone.

A member of St. Joseph's happened to own a boutique in the area, and so for one day, 20 percent of every purchase went directly to Let Them Live to support Ana. At the same time, customers were told they could purchase items and have them sent directly to Ana. (More than a few cute onesies and burp cloths were packed up and shipped to California.) Another day, a group of children from the church set up a lemonade stand and set aside all the profits for Ana. Every week, Father Reynolds would give an update, and the fundraising goal (and the congregation's progress) were placed on a bulletin board in the narthex of the church. This way, everyone knew what was going on and how close they were to achieving their fundraising goal.

Ana wasn't just some stranger in need on the other side of the country, though. Over the months, the members of St. Joseph's came to know her. That sort of thing happens when you decide to love someone. The children sent her cards; the adults sent her letters and called her on the phone. And as the due date drew near, the women of St. Joseph's held Ana a virtual baby shower.

Church members filled up a large shipping box with gifts for Ana and the baby, and then sent it off to Los Angeles. A few days later, at the designated time, Ana logged on to a video conference call to see lots of folks gathered into a church Sunday school room, smiling back at her on her computer monitor. They were all there to love on her. One by one, Ana opened the gifts from St. Joseph's and felt the support she knew she needed when she first contacted Let Them Live. Speaking about the experience later, Ana said she was shocked that this many people—people she had never even met—cared about her and her baby.

A short time later, Ana gave birth to a beautiful, healthy baby girl she named Analis, but not before St. Joseph's kept their commitment to meet her financial needs. It took generosity, hard work, and a commitment not to grow weary in doing good, but that one church, which is neither particularly large nor wealthy, saved a human life and changed Ana's in the process.

Do you know what my favorite part of St. Joseph's story is? I love that it's not unique. The Adopt-a-Mom program has now been tried dozens of times, and everywhere its been tried, its been a success. Communities discover the joy of "doing something" with their pro-life commitment, and moms in need discover people really do care and really do want to help.

Every day, I feel in my shoulders and in my heart just how much work goes into caring for a mom and saving just one life from abortion. I know the only way Let Them Live is going to grow is if we multiply exponentially, training others to do the work we've started. As I've said already, what we're doing isn't complicated. It's actually very simple: we take away the financial struggles that make abortion seem like a mom's only option. It's not rocket science. It's just love in action, with the goal of saving an unborn child. Anyone can do it. And that's why I'm excited to do just that: help *anyone* who wants to be a part of our mission get on board.

At the end of Emily's talk at Stetson, I could tell the air in the room had changed. The hostility that had been there at the start had dissipated some. I should be used to this phenomenon by now, but somehow it always hits me as a pleasant surprise. You see, whenever we get the opportunity to tell people about our work, we invariably make new friends on both sides of the abortion issue.

There will likely always be some people who are hardened pro-choice activists, unwilling to see any path for a woman in need that doesn't lead to an abortionist's table. But many people who consider themselves pro-choice want women to have a genuine choice with their pregnancy. They are more than happy to see moms choose life if that's what they really want. When we explain that what we're doing is giving moms that choice—a choice that simple economics, the hard knocks of life, and the cost of living in America have made more difficult—they want to help.

Let Them Live is a pro-life organization, and we make no apologies about that. But I'm proud to say we have donors and supporters who consider themselves ardently pro-choice. They vote Democratic, and they want to see abortion legal and available in all fifty states. And yet, they see the good we're doing and can't deny the difference we're making. And they've joined us.

It's a beautiful thing to see people on opposing sides of an issue come together to do something good for the world, especially when that good thing is helping women in need and saving lives in the process. Bridging political divides wasn't something we set out to do when we started down this road; it's just a wonderful, unexpected byproduct. But because it's so beautiful, it makes me think we must be on the right path.

If you want to own one of Elon Musk's five hundred Roadsters, you can do so. They can be purchased at auction. If you look hard enough, you might even find one reasonably-priced. But parts are hard to find and are therefore very expensive, so keeping one of those cars on the road is a bit of a challenge. Those first five hundred Roadsters paved the way for something better; but for the most part, they belong to collectors and wealthy car enthusiasts.

Unlike an experimental car, the work of our hands will never be isolated to private collectors. The children we save will grow up to change the world and the moms we help will never be the same. Those moms and their kids will share their stories, changing hearts and minds in the process. With Adopt-a-Mom, we're changing whole communities, too. People are beginning to think differently about what it looks like to be pro-life and what it is to love their neighbor. And as it turns out, we're also changing the culture war a bit, in our own small way. If people who passionately disagree about an issue as contentious as abortion can come together, then anything's possible, isn't it?

CHAPTER 11

A VISION TO TAKE HOLD OF

There wasn't an abortion facility in Sioux Falls that would take her past thirteen weeks, so Mercy sat and waited in the lobby of a Planned Parenthood clinic across the state line in Minnesota. The bus ride had taken more than four hours, but it had been free—paid in full by a pro-choice outfit that lived up to their name: Access for Every Woman.

Mercy was nervous, to put it mildly. She knew it made sense for her to be there. Everyone said so. She already had two children, and with her financial situation what it was, she just couldn't handle another one. Not now, anyway. They had told her "the procedure"—that's what they had called it— would take two days. She didn't like that, of course. She wanted this whole experience to be over already; she didn't want to have to think about what she was doing, or what they'd be doing to her, for two whole days. She wanted it all in her rearview mirror so she could work on moving past this entire season of her life.

If nothing else, waiting rooms are aptly named. Mercy waited and waited, and the longer she waited, the more she began to question if she was really doing the right thing. Then she heard it—the woman in the next room, apparently up on the table, restrained for her own protection, in the middle of an abortion. Mercy could hear her crying, even wailing at times. *Was it really that painful? Is she just now realizing it's too late to change her mind? What are they doing to that poor woman?*

Mercy had been scrolling through Instagram, more out of nervous habit than anything else, but with the anguish coming through the wall, she decided she needed to make sure she wanted this abortion. She searched "abortion help" and found Let Them Live. She sent a single word to our social media coordinator via direct message: "Help." Within a few moments, Mercy's phone chirped. She had received a response. Haley, the Let Them Live employee on the other end of the conversation, told Mercy that "help" is exactly what we were there for. Mercy explained she was at Planned Parenthood, waiting to go in and have an abortion. She didn't feel comfortable explaining her doubts to the woman behind the desk. She didn't think she'd let her just walk out at this point. But she didn't want a confrontation; she just wanted to leave.

"Tell them you have to go to the bathroom. Then we can talk," Haley messaged back. A few minutes later, one of our counselors was on the phone with Mercy. She told her we were there to walk alongside her, that if she didn't really want to have this abortion, we would be there with financial support so she could choose life. A few minutes later, Mercy packed up her things and headed outside to an Uber we called for her. Back at the hotel room, over the next four hours, Mercy shared her needs and her frustrations, her fears and her doubts, and we worked out a plan—together. I'm grateful that, in the end, Mercy chose life and, several months later, gave birth to a beautiful little girl she named Jenna.

I love Mercy's story. Well, in truth I love all our Let Them Live stories—but Mercy's is special for a couple of reasons. First, it's rare that a woman reaches out to us when they're already in the abortion clinic, which just goes to show that the statistics are right: there are many women who choose abortion not because they truly want to but because they don't believe there are any other options. And second, it illustrates just how different Let Them Live is from other pro-life organizations.

From the start, I knew we wanted to be different. One of the things that has always bothered me about the pro-life message—most of it anyhow—is the emphasis on the negative. "Abortion is murder!" We know. And the world knows what we're against. What they really want to know is, *What are you for?*

The pro-abortion left is great at spinning things positively. Ask anyone on the street, and they'll tell you what an organization like Planned Parenthood is in favor of:

- Women's rights
- Women's reproductive health
- The freedom to choose
- A woman's bodily autonomy
- Family planning

It's no wonder there's a general feeling among the most outspoken voices in our culture—politicians, the media, Hollywood celebrities, musicians, and social media influencers—that to be pro-choice is to be a good person. In their minds, and in the minds of those who are just casually paying attention, abortion is a moral good; it's a way of caring for women.

When you stop and think about it, our cultural moment is a bizarre one. People who are in favor of starving the life out of a still-forming child are considered the good guys by most people. Groups who push surgical procedures designed to chemically burn a baby to death in utero somehow have the moral high ground, and those who are fighting for an end to such barbarism are the narrow-minded freedom crushers. It's absolutely insane, but I don't think we've come to this place by accident. Like I said, the pro-choice powerful have done an incredible job of shaping the cultural conversation. But it hasn't helped that those of us on the pro-life side of the argument haven't been vocal with what we're *for*. Most people only hear us shouting about what we're against.

Now, to be fair, there are plenty of pregnancy resource centers across the country doing a superb job caring for the needs of pregnant women during and after their pregnancies. It's amazing work; it's just that they're not particularly loud about it. The loudest voices on the right repeat the familiar refrain about the evils of abortion but are usually pretty quiet about the underlying issues that bring many women to the abortion clinic in the first place.

When Emily and I first started Let Them Live, we decided we wanted to change the conversation. We wanted to be known by what we're for, not what we're against. For starters, we're for:

- Helping women at every stage of pregnancy and afterwards
- Financially and emotionally supporting women in need
- Removing financial obstacles so that women in crisis have a real choice

- Connecting women to a community that will come alongside of them
- Providing tangible support to meet real-life needs

And of course we're for rescuing babies from abortion. While other pro-life groups might approach a pregnant woman who's strongly considering having an abortion and say, "We love you. You don't have to kill your baby," we train our counselors to let each woman share their unique story. We ask, "Why are you having this abortion?" and "What made you decide you needed to have an abortion?" Most of the time, these women will open up to us about what's going on in their life. They'll tell us how they lost their job and they're already three months behind on their rent. They'll let us know about an abusive boyfriend or husband. They'll tell us about underlying medical issues, mistakes from their past, and the doubts that keep them up at night. All this opens a door to a real conversation. Our goal is not merely to talk someone out of an abortion; we want to provide real support so that abortion no longer seems like an attractive option, and we want to set each mom up for success when their baby comes.

Our counselors get the joy of offering these women real hope. They get to say things like, "What if we paid your back rent and made your rent payments for the next three months?" "What if we helped you find a new and better job?" "What if we could connect you to a local community that would come alongside you and provide for some of your most pressing needs?" It's these conversations that change lives. Most of the moms we talk to accept our help and choose life.

Early on in this book, I shared a statistic gleaned from a study by the Guttmacher Institute. A full 73% of women choose abortion primarily for financial reasons. That means that nearly three quarters of all abortions in the United States could be prevented if we just supplied the necessary funding. In 2020, there were 930,160 abortions performed in the United States.[1] Of those 930,160 abortions, roughly 679,017, or 73%, might not have happened if the moms involved had received some financial relief.

By studying our own work, I've discovered that 89% of the abortion-determined women who are referred to us end up choosing life. That means that of those 679,017 women who had an abortion because of financial need, 604,325 would not have done so if they had connected with Let Them Live. That's 604,325 babies saved (plus several more when you add twins and triplets into the mix). We may not be able to stop every abortion from taking place, but our model of personal support and financial assistance could put an end to most of them. You may remember from an earlier chapter that Let Them Live spends an average of $13,944 to support a mom. That means that for around $8.4 billion a year, we could make sure that no child dies in the womb in the United States because of financial hardship.

I know—$8.4 billion. That's *billion* with a *B*. It's a big number, but it's not insurmountable. To put all this in perspective, think about this: according to the 2020 census, there were 258,343,281 adults living in the US[2], and Gallup tells us that 39% of US adults consider themselves pro-life[3]—that's 100,753,880 men and women over the age of eighteen who say they believe in the right to life for the unborn. If every one of these self-described pro-life individuals decided to take a stand and help us reach the $8.4 billion goal, each one would need to commit just $83.63 to the fight per year. That's less than $7 per month—considerably less than the price of Netflix. Obviously, giving ability varies from person to person, but all this math reveals it's not an impossible dream to think we can end need-driven abortion in this country. Changing the world is within our grasp. We just need to spread the vision and make it happen.

I don't expect to raise a billion dollars this year, let alone $8.4 billion. I don't expect we'll do it next year either. We won't do it in five years or even ten. But my hope and prayer is that, within my lifetime, Let Them Live and similar organizations will raise enough money so that no mom feels she needs to choose abortion because of the financial obstacles in her life. And here's the beautiful thing: this isn't an all-or-nothing proposition. Every life we save matters, so as we grow and gain support, we'll save lots and lots of lives. We win every time a mom chooses life instead of the abortion clinic. Every time.

Just a few years ago, Mercy's story would have been impossible. Before mobile phones, she would have been in the waiting room of that Planned Parenthood with no way to reach the outside world. Before social media sites like Instagram, she wouldn't have had a way to send Let Them Live a direct message and ask for help. Before Uber, we couldn't have sent a car to pick her up within minutes. These days, we take technology like this for granted, but it's incredibly powerful. That's why we're committed to leveraging technology to help as many moms as possible.

Years ago, when I offered Debbie twelve hundred and fifty dollars to cancel her appointment at the abortion clinic, it was technology that made all the difference. I had connected with Debbie's cousin Abbie over Facebook. Abbie and Debbie texted back and forth in real time. I then sent my payment—everything we had in our bank account at the time—using the PayPal app on my smartphone. Then, when I realized Emily and I probably weren't the only ones who would give financially to save a life, we started crowdfunding to raise money for Debbie and moms just like her using GoFundMe.

At every step, we've reached further than would've otherwise been possible because of technology. Let Them Live is nimble and responsive to the needs of our moms, no matter where they live in the country, because of the tools at our disposal. At the same time (and in just a matter of seconds), for every mom we serve, we're able to reach thousands of like-minded souls who want to get on board and help. We're also able to tell the stories of the moms we support and the babies we save, sharing video testimonials with tens of millions of people worldwide. And we're not stopping yet.

Our iFundLife.org site allows anyone—and that *anyone* includes you—to launch their own crowdfunding campaign in support of a Let Them Live mom. By reaching out to their circle of influence, supporters expand our reach and raise awareness of our cause, all the while helping a mom in need and saving a baby in the process. There are organizations whose sole purpose is to raise money to fund abortions, so we're taking them on, one donor at a time. Our #IFundLife campaign was birthed because there is a huge need to grow our financial resources to keep up with and outpace the competing abortion-funding organizations.

Soon, we'll be launching the OneLife subscription app (and by the time you're reading this, it may already be a reality). For about the cost of Netflix, people who want to support the work of Let Them Live on a monthly basis will receive access to an app that provides a special stream of content they can view and share on their own social media platforms. The app also serves as a personalized community organizing platform. We want to see Let Them Live's supporters joining together to adopt moms in their area, crowdfund for specific needs, and connect with one another in real time. Subscribers will also be able to direct their monthly donations to specific moms and donate additional funds as needs arise, should they choose to do so. OneLife will give people who want to walk with us on this journey special behind-the-scenes access and a seat at the table. Giving is one thing; becoming a part of a movement is quite another, and this app is a step in that direction.

~

I hope you've caught a vision for what we're trying to do at Let Them Live. If so, and you'd like to join us in our mission, here are some ways you can get involved today:

Volunteer

As you know, our goal at Let Them Live is to connect with as many moms as possible to save as many babies as we can. On average, fifteen to twenty moms reach out to us each week, looking for help. We want to empower these moms and give them confidence and hope so they know abortion is not their only option. This is made possible, in large part, through our incredible team of volunteer pregnancy counselors.

If counseling isn't for you, we can always use help with our Gratitude Program, a volunteer-run operation to say thank you to our generous donors. At more than one hundred volunteers and counting, the Gratitude Program is a crucial part of Let Them Live's mission. For every donation Let Them Lives receives, a volunteer writes and mails a personalized thank-you card. It's just a small way to show our appreciation. These cards also serve to remind our donors about our important work, and as a result, they help us raise more money and save more lives from abortion.

The Heartbeat Club

We love it when our donors who see a specific need jump in to help with a one-time gift. But without the support of donors who give regularly, month after month, Let Them Live's work would not be sustainable in the long term. By choosing to give monthly, you'll provide security for Let Them Live moms and empower our team to provide immediate support for women in crisis.

Further, by becoming a Heartbeat Club Member, you'll join a proactive community committed to helping moms choose life for their babies. You'll also stay up to date on Let Them Live news with our quarterly newsletter, and you'll be able to proudly show off your support with our Heartbeat Club welcome package and special gifts.

Adopt-a-Mom

As mentioned, the Adopt-a-Mom program is a platform for churches, pro-life organizations, and philanthropists to empower abortion-determined women to confidently choose life for their babies. Let Them Live matches Adopt-a-Mom sponsors to a specific mom experiencing a crisis pregnancy. Sponsors agree to financially provide the necessary life-saving resources so that she doesn't feel pressured to have an abortion.

Sponsors follow their adopted mom's pregnancy milestones through updates, ultrasound images, and any photos of her precious baby sent to Let Them Live after the little one is born. Funds raised through Adopt-a-Mom sponsorship are used to furnish 24/7 counseling services, housing and rent payments, groceries and other necessities, car and transportation payments, and financial and job-related counseling.

Social Media Ambassador

Use your social media platform to save lives. As a Let Them Live Social Media Ambassador, you'll play a critical role in spreading Let Them Live's message to moms in crisis pregnancies and prospective new supporters.

Let Them Live has cracked the code on how to help women in crisis pregnancies. Now, we need your help getting the message out. Let Them Live Ambassadors receive helpful content and materials to start conversations, updates about moms and babies currently being supported, access to the Let Them Live Ambassador Facebook group, and behind-the-scenes insights about Let Them Live.

If you'd like to learn more about Let Them Live or get involved, visit letthemlive.org. You can also email us at info@letthemlive.org or call us at (260) 200-3789. We have a lot of work ahead of us, but Emily and I are excited for what the future holds. We'd love for you to join us!

NOTES

I. TO SAVE A LIFE

1. Lawrence B. Finer, Lori F. Frohwirth, Lindsay A. Dauphinee, Susheela Singh, and Ann M. Moore, "Reasons U.S. Women Have Abortions," *Perspectives on Sexual and Reproductive Health* 37, no. 3 (September 2005): 110–118. https://www.guttmacher.org/journals/psrh/2005/reasons-us-women-have-abortions-quantitative-and-qualitative-perspectives.

II. A VISION TO TAKE HOLD OF

1. Rachel K. Jones, Jesse Philbin, Marielle Kirstein, Elizabeth Nash, Kimberley Lufkin, "Long-Term Decline in US Abortions Reverses, Showing Rising Need for Abortion as Supreme Court Is Poised to Overturn Roe v. Wade," Guttmacher Institute, June 15, 2022, https://www.guttmacher.org/article/2022/06/long-term-decline-us-abortions-reverses-showing-rising-need-abortion-supreme-court.
2. Stella U. Ogunwole, Megan A. Rabe, Andrew W. Davids, and Zoe Caplan, "U.S. Adult Population Grew Faster Than Nation's Total Population From 2010 to 2020," United States Census Bureau, August 12, 2021, https://www.census.gov/library/stories/2021/08/united-states-adult-population-grew-faster-than-nations-total-population-from-2010-to-2020.html.
3. "'Pro-Choice' or 'Pro-Life' Demographic Table," Gallup, May 22, 2022, https://news.gallup.com/poll/244709/pro-choice-pro-life-2018-demographic-tables.aspx.

ABOUT THE AUTHORS

Nathan & Emily Berning are the co-founders of Let Them Live, a 501(c)(3) non-profit organization dedicated to saving lives from abortion by providing financial support, counseling and coaching to women considering abortion.

Prior to founding Let Them Live, Nathan worked for Dr. Ben Carson's 2016 Presidential Campaign as the AskBen Director. He led a team that answered hundreds of thousands of questions and sent millions of texts and emails to Dr. Carson's supporters. He also built technology in both the political and tech worlds.

Prior to founding Let Them Live, Emily graduated with a degree in Biology from Colorado State University in 2017. While at CSU, she started a Students for Life chapter and dedicated her life to the pro-life movement. In 2019, she officially abandoned her dreams of becoming an OB/GYN to build Let Them Live full time.

ALSO BY EMILY BERNING

Shout Your Abortion Too
Compiled & Edited by Emily Berning